News as Hegemonic Reality

NEWS AS HEGEMONIC REALITY

American Political Culture and the Framing of News Accounts

Allan Rachlin

PRAEGER

New York
Westport, Connecticut
London

Library of Congress Cataloging-in-Publication Data

Rachlin, Allan.
    News as hegemonic reality : American political culture and the framing of news accounts / Allan Rachlin.
        p.   cm.
    Includes index.
    ISBN 0-275-92534-X (alk. paper)
    1. Press and politics—United States.   2. Political culture—United States.   3. Foreign news—United States.   4. United States—Politics and government—1945–   I. Title.
E839.5.R34   1988
302.2'32'0973—dc 19   88-12009

Copyright © 1988 by Praeger Publishers

All rights reserved. No portion of this book may be reproduced, by any process or technique, without the express written consent of the publisher.

Library of Congress Catalog Card Number: 88-12009
ISBN: 0-275-92534-X

First published in 1988

Praeger Publishers, One Madison Avenue, New York, NY 10010
A division of Greenwood Press, Inc.

Printed in the United States of America

The paper used in this book complies with the Permanent Paper Standard issued by the National Information Standards Organization (Z39.48-1984).

10   9   8   7   6   5   4   3   2   1

TO VICKI

                                for more than I sometimes care to admit

CONTENTS

1	Introduction	1
2	Studying the Press	5
3	KAL 007	35
4	Solidarity	93
5	Conclusion	123

Appendix A: Primary Focus of *New York Times*
Articles about Poland and Solidarity 137

Appendix B: A Note on Methods 139

Selected Bibliography 145

Index 149

News as Hegemonic Reality

1
INTRODUCTION

In his classic article, "Social Control in the Newsroom: A Functional Analysis," Breed (1955) suggested that a newspaper is the product of socialization into the organization that is experienced by all participants. White (1950) has suggested that the presentation of the news has been shaped by strategically located gatekeepers within each news organization, while Tuchman (1972) has cited the "strategic ritual" of objectivity as the basis of the structure of news stories. Others have suggested that either the physical limitations of print media (Rock 1973) or the business considerations of the news industry (Sterling 1973) shape the presentation of news. There has even been the suggestion that journalists' fantasies, either of a general audience (Pool and Schulman 1964) or of an audience of other journalists (Darnton 1975) influence the manner in which news is presented.

While these theories of the formation of news accounts can each contribute to our understanding of the presentation of news, they do not address the issues of the press in a larger social environment. They do not explore the mutually formative relationship of the press and the social order or the issue of how well the press serves one of its most important assumed functions in America—its service to democracy.

THE DEMOCRATIC ASSUMPTION

It has been suggested (for example, Altschull 1984) that a fundamental assumption of the American citizen is that democracy thrives in our nation, at least in part because of the information made available to the public by the news media. An informed public, it is assumed, is required for successful representative democracy. That public can best be served by a news media that enables it to develop informed opinions and reasoned choices. "One of the most powerful hopes advanced by theories of representative government is that news media remain free so that they can educate the public in making political choices" (Clark and Fredin 1978:143). Altschull (1984:19) summarizes "the democratic assumption" in the following manner:

> In a democracy, it is the people who rule. The voice of the people is heard in the voting booths. The decisions made by the people in the voting booth are based on the information made available to them. That information is provided primarily by the news media. Hence, the news media are indispensable to the survival of democracy.

Supreme Court Justice Learned Hand indicated that the democratic assumption was woven into the fabric of our Constitution when he wrote that the newspaper industry

> serves one of the most vital of all general interests—the dissemination of news from as many different sources and with as many different faces as possible. That interest is akin to, if indeed it is not the same as, the interest protected by the First Amendment; it presupposes that right conclusions are more likely to be gathered out of a multitude of tongues, than through any kind of authoritarian selection. To many this is, and always will be, folly; but we have staked upon it our all. (cited in Porter 1981:98)

Justice Hand was expressing faith in Milton's self-righting principle just as Thomas Jefferson did when he observed "that truth is great and will prevail if left to herself, that she is the proper and sufficient antagonist to error, and has nothing to fear from conflict" (cited in Altschull 1984:21).

To use a colloquialism of capitalism, democracy requires an open and free marketplace of ideas and perspectives. In such a marketplace competition and contentiousness serve the interest of perfection as we use the alternative views provided for us in the press to challenge and improve each other's understanding. Understanding and vision are sharpened on the whetstone of unfettered debate. It is through such debate that the public is able to (correctly) identify meritorious views. The competition among the press serves as a "gyroscopic force" (Hulteng 1981:222) which maintains the media on a responsible heading and enables the public to distinguish true, reliable information from that which is false or misleading. The unrestrained press then guarantees our ability to draw right conclusions as it assures us of reliable information upon which we can base our judgments.

The tradition of a free press that enables informed debate is recognized by the public as an essential requirement of democracy. It is in the shared value of an unrestrained press that we find a consensus more fundamental than that found in any shared conclusions. Consensus in mass democracies may not be found in even the most essential substantive issues, but instead in "the established habit of intercommunication, of discussion, debate, negotiation and compromise, and the toleration of heresies, or even of indifference, up to the point of 'clear and present danger' which threatens the life of society itself'' (Wirth 1948:9). Again, it is the free, unfettered exchange of ideas that is understood to be fundamental to our society. More than substantive agreement, it is the manner in which we come to conclusions, in which we communicate with each other, that characterizes our mass democratic society. It is a free press that permits such communication.

JOURNALISM WITHIN HEGEMONY

If indeed a free press is necessary to provide the communication that is indispensable to the survival of democracy, we need examine our own press, the forces that guide it, and evaluate its contribution to democracy. Does the American press, protected legally from the influence and constraints of government control, with journalists guided by principles of objectivity, maximize democratic possibilities, or must we instead understand these legal and professional claims to be made within a particular social context and to serve the requirements of a particular social order?

We can best understand how the press serves the needs of democracy—or fails to do so—by expanding our study of the press beyond the organizational and journalistic issues identified by Breed, White, Tuchman, and the rest, to include a broader political sociology that places the examination of the press (or the entire news media more generally) in a social context beyond individual organizations or the journalistic profession. Such a study would recognize the press to be immersed in the totality of social relationships, both influenced by and influencing the history of our social relationships. Rather than standing apart from the world on which it reports, the press is instead understood to be of that world.

By examining the presentation in the press of selected events (a poor term, as it indicates an occurrence that can be isolated in time) and by looking at the pattern of presentation over time and then comparing key aspects of the presentation of different events, fundamental assumptions will be identified that serve to provide the "frames" (Tuchman 1978; Gitlin 1980) or contexts within which the events are presented. The assumptions and consequential frames will be shown to originate not in organizational or professional concerns but instead within political culture, society's dominant world view, the hegemonic order. Taken beyond the more narrow concerns of organization and profession, the political significance of the press's presentation of the world will become more apparent. Indeed, to be fully understood, the organizational and professional concerns themselves must be seen to exist within the framework of a larger social order. Once acknowledged, the relationship between news media and that social order can be better examined and understood.

It is the purpose of this study to explore that relationship. More specifically, it is intended to examine the role of political culture or hegemonic ideology in defining journalistic accounts of the world. A press free from legal constraints imposed by an oppressive government can still undermine the possibility of pluralism and the requirements of democracy, if it is constrained instead by a narrow vision of the world that reproduces existing social relationships by inhibiting the possibility of realizing or even imagining alternative realities. It is one purpose of this project to determine whether the American press is so constrained and therefore a force that undermines rather than promotes democracy. It is a further purpose, if such constraint can be documented, to understand the nature of that narrow vision that inhibits democratic choice.

REFERENCES

Altschull, J. Herbert (1984) *Agents of Power: The Role of the News Media in Human Affairs* (White Plains, NY: Longman).

Breed, Walter (1955) "Social Control in the Newsroom," *Social Forces* 33:326–35.

Clark, Peter, and Eric Fredin (1978) "Newspapers, Television and Political Reasoning," *Public Opinion Quarterly* 42:143–60.

Darnton, Robert (1975) "Writing News and Telling Stories," *Daedalus* 104:175–94.

Gitlin, Todd (1980) *The Whole World is Watching* (Berkeley, CA: University of California Press).

Hulteng, John L. (1981) "Holding the Media Accountable," in *What's News: The Media in American Society*, edited by Elie Abel (San Francisco, CA: Institute for Contemporary Studies), pp. 211–32.

Pool, Ithiel de Sola, and Irwin Schulman (1964) "Newsmen's Fantasies, Audiences and Newswriting," in *People, Society and Mass Communications*, edited by L.A. Dexter and D.M. White (New York: Free Press), pp. 143–59.

Porter, William E. (1981) "The Media Baronies: Bigger, Fewer, More Powerful," in *What's News: The Media in American Society*, edited by Elie Abel (San Francisco: Institute for Contemporary Studies), pp. 97–115.

Rock, Paul (1973) "News as Eternal Recurrence," in *The Manufacture of News: Social Problems, Deviance and the Mass Media*, edited by Stanley Cohen and Jack Young (London: Anchor Press), pp. 73–80.

Sterling, Christopher H. (1973) "Some Basic Limitations in Mass News," in *Mass News: Practices, Controversies and Alternatives*, edited by D.J. LeRoy and C.H. Sterling (Englewood Cliffs, NJ: Prentice-Hall), pp. 70–79.

Tuchman, Gaye (1972) "Objectivity as Strategic Ritual: An Examination of Newsmen's Notions of Objectivity," *American Journal of Sociology* 77:660–79.

——— (1978) *Making News: A Study in the Construction of Reality* (New York: Free Press).

White, David M. (1950) "The 'Gatekeeper': A Case Study in Selection of News," *Journalism Quarterly* 27:383–90.

Wirth, Louis (1948) "Consciousness and Mass Communication," *American Sociological Review* 13:1–15.

2

STUDYING THE PRESS

JOURNALISM AS PATRIOTISM

A free press and unfettered discussion of public issues provide the bedrock of democratic societies. The democratic assumption claims the news media, as a conduit of necessary information, is indispensable to democracy as it permits the people to speak with a knowledgeable voice and to make educated choices. Despite such claims, and the further assertion that the accomplishment of such preconditions has permitted the realization of democracy in American society, the suggestion has also been made that it might be justified to limit the multitude of tongues at some time or even to silence some tongues all the time. Debate and heresy are tolerated only up to a point. When a threat to society, to the established social order, is perceived, discussion is terminated. Free discussion is simply a means, albeit the most effective, to identify "correct" conclusions. It is the conclusions that have primacy and not free discussion. If some voices are to be silenced because they present a clear and present danger to society and social order, then it is that society and social order that must be recognized to be of primary value. The importance of order then does not originate in its guarantees of freedom, including the freedom of debate; its primacy instead originates in order itself. The press, by these accounts, is not to be absolutely unfettered but instead to maintain a bias that supports the maintenance of society.

Henry (1981:153) acknowledges that "ultimately all journalism is patriotism," but defends this fact by observing that journalists express their patriotic devotion in alternative manners. While some journalists believe that their shared goal is furthered by "building respect for leaders, institutions, social order and law enforcement," others believe the same goal is supported by fostering an "adversary process" that challenges cherished institutions and arrangements (Henry 1981:153). Henry also notes that there are limitations to the diversity acceptable in the free press of a democratic society. He observes that "whatever the normal detachment, in times of crisis reporters spontaneously become nationalists. In the early days of the Iran hostage trouble, print—and especially broadcast—reporters, including the networks, readied us for war" (1981:272). Unless Henry can identify how the hostage situation was a crisis that presented an immediate danger to the stability of American society, this example seems to indicate a shared willingness of journalists to engage in war hysteria rather than a commitment to maintain journalistic detachment. Unless Henry can identify the democratic significance of the spontaneous patriotic fervor, this example seems to indicate a shared understanding of nationalist interest rather than a commitment to democracy.[1] Henry has shown us a press more uniform than dissident and more committed to a nationalist agenda than democratic debate. It seems that, like Henry, journalists have assumed an identity of democracy and patriotism. It seems also that they assume the meaning of the concepts themselves to be apparent and beyond contention.

These characterizations of the press suggest fundamental issues that need to be addressed regarding journalism and the news media in this society. Given the stated commitment to a free press and uninhibited debate, how can constraints be justified even during times of crisis? How do journalists come to identify a time as one of crisis and "spontaneously" become nationalists? More fundamentally, is all journalism ultimately patriotism? That is, even during times of normalcy, when the shared concern for crisis is absent, is there a shared conception of the world that is expressed in the mass media that serves to uphold the existing social order? If this commonality in time of normalcy exists, what is its source and what is its content? Does it originate in the psychology of individual journalists, the demands of journalistic organizations or the profession, or the nature of our societal environment? What are the specific values that are shared and championed in accounts of journalists? What institutions or institutional arrangements are bolstered by those values? It is these questions that are addressed in this work.

If the labor of journalists is ultimately of nationalistic character, such labor, it seems, might be understood to violate the canon of objectivity. Such a violation would indicate conflict between the norms that are said to guide journalists and actual journalistic practice. Before directly considering questions about the existence, the origin, and the content of a nationalistic press, it would be helpful to consider what is meant by the journalistic concept of objectivity. We can then consider journalistic practice in light of journalistic values.

JOURNALISTIC OBJECTIVITY

Though a standard of objectivity might be understood to guide journalistic activity, it seems that there is no single, unchallenged meaning of the concept.

A brief consideration of a variety of efforts to understand what is meant by objectivity and its application to news journalism will provide a context for further discussion of journalistic news accounts and the manner in which the world is presented in the news media.

Accuracy

A classic approach to the study of objectivity focuses on the issue of accuracy. In an early study, Charnley (1936) sent questionnaires to the principals of stories in three Minneapolis daily newspapers. Charnley's respondents reported errors in almost half of the stories, with errors in meaning, names, and titles being most frequent. He found that stories were more likely to be reported accurately when they were written from prepared material than when the reporter was more involved in the fact gathering. He concluded that his method of determining newspaper accuracy—verifying stories with those actors who are named in the accounts—was "basically sound" (1936:401). Charnley assumed that accuracy could be measured by determining the degree of correspondence between a news account and the real world or what really happened. The way to know about the real world was, apparently, to ask the people who were identified as having taken part in the event reported. While many others have followed Charnley's effort to determine the correspondence of news accounts to the real world, their methods and results have varied.

Scanlon (1972), recognizing possible problems in relying on the voluntary mail response of event participants, as well as the objectivity of those who do respond, has sought to determine the accuracy of accounts by re-covering stories. He found, as Charnley had 36 years earlier, that story accuracy was increased as reporter participation was minimized. Scanlon observed that "the fastest route to an error is to allow a reporter to get involved—by an interview or a dialogue of any sort" (1972:589). When the types of errors made in an account were considered, Scanlon determined that the most serious ones occurred when the reporter had no contact at all with the story. He therefore concluded that a journalist must understand the attitude of a news source toward the event reported and that significant errors in news accounts could be minimized by having reporters specialize in particular subjects.

In more recent efforts to re-cover news stories, Scanlon (1978) reported the development of the Emergency Communication Research Unit with which he and his colleagues have been able to be at the scene of emergency/disaster events within 24 hours of their initial occurrence. Using the research unit, Scanlon determined that while there were errors in detail due to the haste with which reports were constructed, the general impression communicated in the coverage of six events in Canada was correct. A simple count of errors then does not indicate the truthfulness of a news report or series of reports. Objectivity, accuracy, and truthfulness seem to be more subtle and complicated matters than first realized.

Bias

Accuracy, or the lack of it, is often considered to be a measure of bias in the news. Inaccuracy here is understood to represent a systematic distortion of reality that presents not only an untrue picture of reality but a consistently patterned untrue picture.

At a time when Vice President Spiro Agnew was prominent in the news, in part because of his attacks on the media, the coverage he received was the subject of much study. Treatment of Agnew in the press was used as a measure of news bias. Meyer (1972) had students view a debate in which Agnew took part or read accounts of the debate from the *New York Times*. Finding that readers judged Agnew more harshly than did the viewers, Meyer concluded that the *Times*'s story on the debate was biased. In a more exhaustive study, Coffey (1975) found the matter less simply summarized. Using three methods of content analysis, Coffey attempted to identify a quantitative measure of bias in the reporting of political news. Combining the use of a simple column-inch count, Budd's attention score, and Stempel's headline classification, Coffey examined coverage of electoral politics. He was able to conclude that "overall the coverage given the two parties was virtually equal" (1975:552). He added, though, that there appears to be a "strong probability that political news reporting was affected by management attitudes" (1975:553).

Studies of television journalism similarly indicate no clear uniform assessment of the existence or nature of bias. A study of the network's coverage of the 1968 presidential election (Weaver 1972) concluded that the networks saw the election process as an event rather than as an issue. Consequently the matter of fairness in treatment of political alternatives seemed inappropriate. Weaver does conclude though, that while there was no evidence of a political bias of journalists, candidate Richard Nixon did face a "journalistic" bias created by how the event was structured by the networks.

Another study (Russo 1971), at about the same time, looked at coverage of the Vietnam War. It concluded that coverage on CBS and NBC was unbiased. However, Russo notes that until the fall of 1969 there was no mention of civilian casualties in the war. Then at about the same time, both networks began to make frequent mention of such casualties. Both the initial failure to note the casualties and the later attention to the matter seem to require explanation. Does the change indicate a change in the nature of the war or modification in the media's representation of the war? Keeley (1971), again writing at about the same time, attempts to document a political bias that permeates all network television. In *The Left-Leaning Antenna*, Keeley finds liberals and radicals using their positions in the networks to distort systematically the world and mislead us. Finally on this matter, a study of the next presidential election in 1972 (Hofstetter 1976) found network coverage of candidates, parties, and issues to be neither politically nor structurally biased.

In an effort to summarize the literature on media bias, Stevenson and Greene

(1980) conclude that most studies of media coverage of parties or candidates seldom find a systematic slant to the reporting. In a "common sense" approach to the issue of bias, Bartley (1981), noting dissatisfaction within both government and business organizations with their press coverage, concludes that claims of bias represent "an interaction of audience and format" (1981:193). This concurs with the suggestion of Stevenson and Greene "that what news consumers often see as bias in news are cognitive discrepancies between what the news tells them about the political world around them and what they already believe about that world" (1980:118). Bias then, for these analysts, is less a quality of news accounts or the work of news journalists than it is a feeling of dissonance experienced by a public whose ideas of the world are confronted by the reality of the world. Claims of bias then indicate a psychological state and not a characterization or evaluation of the relationship of news accounts to the world. The presentation of news, from this perspective, is assumed to be unproblematic.

The position of Stevenson and Greene is most explicit when they identify three conceptual problems with the traditional approach to the study of news bias (1980:116). First, they suggest that if we are to understand the consumers' perception of bias, we must attend not simply to the object of the account, but to who the consumer is as well. Next, they argue, to understand the level of generalization at which bias is claimed, the consumers need to be asked for specific instances of bias rather than their general perception of it. Finally, they suggest, the cognitive behavioral response of consumers must be observed as they encounter what they see to be specific instances of bias. It appears that when Stevenson and Greene define bias as "the failure to treat all voices in the marketplace of ideas equally," they are addressing an issue of the failure of consumers and not any failure of the news media. The issue is no longer the existence or nature of bias in the news but instead the nature of perception of the news. Clearly, the diversity of perceptions is an interesting and important issue from the perspective of social psychology, but if a recognition of the diversity of perceptions of the media denies a recognition of the nature of the news media, it is a disservice of devastating proportions to an effort to understand our social and political world.

Objectivity as Strategic Ritual

It seems that we have made little progress in an effort to identify what is meant by objectivity in the construction, examination, or evaluation of news. Early efforts to determine the veracity of reports have led to the subsequent recognition that accuracy "in its classical sense" (Scanlon 1972:587) may be too limiting. Studies of news media bias seem to lead to contradictory assessments of its existence and even its direction. In some work, consideration of bias has led to an almost exclusive consideration of the news audience rather than the news organizations and their products.

Weaver's study of the 1968 elections, the work of Gans (1972), and that of

Tuchman (1972), along with the work of others begin to permit an informed examination of the nature of news media and the meaning of objectivity.

Weaver (1972:59) has claimed that those in the media defend their legitimacy by claiming fairness, by which they mean a lack of bias. "[W]rapped in a mantle of 'fairness,' the media indignantly rebuke their critics as 'biased,' 'extremist,' 'self-seeking,' 'manipulative,' or possessed of an irrational desire to punish the innocent messenger who bears the distasteful truth." It is the journalists' recognition, according to Weaver, of both their power and their vulnerability that motivates them to defend their legitimacy.

They do so by claiming their "professional" and "fair" use of the power. By this they mean that their intention and, in general, their achievement is to give equal time, equal space, and equally considerate attention to all popular candidates and all popular views on all popular issues. The media recognize that this strategy will not protect them from the wrath of political extremes, whose views and candidates they systematically ignore. But they do hope it will prevent them from offending the great majority, who presumably will see in the formula of "fairness" at least a rough approximation to "objectivity." (Weaver 1972:59)

Gans (1972) has also noted how the continued use of traditional practices has permitted journalists to effectively limit and cope with criticism.

Such observations have led Tuchman (1972) to term objectivity a "strategic ritual." Objectivity again is not simply a quality of the journalists' product. Neither is it a feature of a reader's or viewer's emotional or psychological predisposition. Instead, "objectivity refers to routine procedures which may be exemplified as formal attributes... and which protect the professional from mistakes and from his critics. It appears the word 'objectivity' is being used defensively as a strategic ritual" (Tuchman 1972:678).[2]

The ritual serves defensive needs of the profession and within the profession. It protects journalists and journalistic organizations from public criticism and protects journalists positions *vis-à-vis* other journalists. Adherence to ritual permits journalists to defend themselves from criticism from peers and from superiors within the organizational hierarchy. Tuchman further notes that the ritual of objectivity facilitates the daily requirements of the journalistic enterprise by allowing deadlines to be met and interorganizational relationships to remain stable.

The Constituents of Objectivity

In a discussion of the meaning and operationalization of the concept of objectivity, Westerstahl (1983), in apparent agreement with Tuchman, writes that "maintaining objectivity in the dissemination of news can... be defined as adherence to certain norms or standards.... It is not a question of basing conclusions on some definition of the inherent nature of objectivity" (Westerstahl

1983:403). Objectivity then exists as a set of norms for journalists to follow and not as an order that shapes the structure of reality. Westerstahl has attempted to clarify the content and operationalization of the norms by providing a schematic representation of the major components of objectivity (1983:404–5). Objectivity "requires," for Westerstahl, factuality and impartiality. Factuality is satisfied by the subrequirements of truth and relevance. Impartiality is satisfied by the subrequirements of balance/nonpartisanship and neutrality of position.

As is frequently the case with efforts to clarify the meaning of problematic concepts, Westerstahl's attempt to identify what is meant by objectivity, though helpful, is itself problematic. Terms such as "truth," "relevance," "balance," and "neutrality" are themselves subject to vague and often contentious meaning. Westerstahl seems to only partially recognize this. He notes, for example, that news items from opposing or various sides cannot always be matched on strict observance of the requirement of balance. He suggests though, that the "more limited requirement" of nonpartisanship can, in such circumstances, be substituted for balance. Acknowledging difficulty in the application of the standard of objectivity, Westerstahl observes that the criteria need to be complemented by an interest theory that would permit the weighing of the significance of various news items. Such consideration would enable judgment to be made concerning the intent not only of individual news stories but also of alternatives.

The meaning of objectivity, as Westerstahl begins to identify it, exists within a context—a social context. Indeed, even the importance of the concept and its centrality to the journalistic endeavor is a social, and therefore historical, phenomenon. It has been suggested that

The goal of "objectivity" was one that did not even occur to the Founders, for there did not exist in the press of that era any publisher or editor who did not see his journal as an instrument for spreading good, or Truth, and not merely as a catalog of points of view. (Altschull 1984:28)

Objectivity, then, is not some state of absolute perfection that the public demands and toward which journalists strive. It is not a quality or attribute that exists as a universal Platonic form. It is a social construction with meaning and importance, influenced by a historical social reality. Professional, political, and commercial (Schudson 1978; Schiller 1981) factors have shaped the development of the newspaper industry and the consequent demands made of journalists and the media. Journalists, rather than being detached, are, like the readers, immersed in the social sea of our culture. The work of journalists is shaped and defined by the currents and tides of that culture.

JOURNALISM AS CULTURAL ACTIVITY

Journalism then, rather than serving as a mirror of society (as is the suggestion of the "accuracy school" of objectivity), is part of society. As such, it will be shown, journalists and journalism are subject to the same forces that press upon the rest of us in our work and daily life. The "mirror theory" of journalism rests on the problematic assumption that

> a dividing line can be drawn between "reality" or society on the one hand and the world of representations on the other. It implies that the media are secondary and derivative, somehow less real than the "real" they reflect, existing above society and passively mirroring it rather than forming an active and integral part of it. (Bennett 1982a:287)

Journalists have been socialized, like most of us, within our culture. They have been exposed to the same constellation of understandings and values as most of us. That exposure has, for the most part, been exclusive of other constellations of world understandings and values. Like the journalists themselves, journalistic institutions are integrated within society. Their societal integration requires them to be responsive to the same social forces that press on all institutions. The press then is unavoidably of reality, of our social context, not removed or detached from it.

Journalistic convention is frequently explained in terms of demands required by organizational (see White 1950; Breed 1955a, 1955b, for classic statements of this position) and professional (Tuchman 1972; Weaver 1972) interest. The practice of journalists, in this view, might present a skewed picture of the world, but this is an unintentional and unavoidable consequence of professional organizational activity. The recognition that the work of journalists is part of, rather than simply a representation of, reality, belies this notion of organizational determinism.

"[T]he daily agenda of reports produced by the media and called 'news' is not the inevitable product of chance events"; rather it is, as has often been suggested, simply "the result of decisions made within news organizations" (Epstein 1981:119). To suggest such organizational determinism is to only recognize the later stages of organizing or "processing" that is done to make the world fit the news. It is obviously true that time constraints such as deadlines, the assignment of reporters to stories and beats, and other apparent requirements of organizational coordination influence the recognition, selection, and telling of news stories. But these organizational imperatives originate in the demands of particular organizational forms, and the events identified as newsworthy represent a statement not only of what sells or what will fit the confines of a report, but also of what is seen to be of importance or interest in a culture that requires selling and that mandates product conformity to the broadest appeal as demanded by commercial interests.

Gans (1972:702) has observed that it is "unquestioned cultural or political assumptions and values" that underlie the descriptive facts that form news reports. Reporters must organize the facts that they gather. They use the common sense "covert assumptions and value judgments" of society in the organizing process. Common sense, or myth (Barthes 1973) in the form of stereotypes, enables reporters and editors to go about their daily routines. Bartley (1981:194) explains how an editor manages through stereotypes. "He has in his mind certain metaphors or themes he will use to organize the news, and he imposes those pre-existing structures upon reality." Bartley then adds, "This does not mean the press is mendacious. This is the *only* way a day's events can conceivably be sorted out and organized by a night's deadline." While imposition of order might be the only conceivable way to meet organizational deadlines, the order imposed by the common sense of a particular culture, its myths, is not the only way in which the world might be conceived.

Weaver has recognized the significance of the manner in which order is imposed upon the day's events, but sees the consequences as unavoidable.

[N]ews itself, as conventionally defined by the journalistic profession has its own structural biases. This means that insofar as we rely on news in forming our mental picture of what is going on in the world, what we are receiving is not a neutral body of information, but rather gathered and presented to illustrate certain ways of seeing the world, based on certain values and favorable to certain courses of action. If so, one issue which arises immediately is that of legitimacy: By what right do the news media propagate their own distinctive vision, which is not entirely neutral as between different candidates, or different sorts of opinions? But that, I fear is an insoluble question. *Any* body of knowledge possesses its bias. (1972:73)

While it is true that any knowledge entails bias, or rather perspective, a particular way of seeing the world, the issue that Weaver avoids here is the monopolization of a particular perspective. Why must news be "conventionally defined"? A common response is that "the stereotypes that order news coverage come from the common coin of society. The stereotypes most useful in communicating with readers or viewers are those the readers or viewers already share" (Bartley 1981:195). However, this ignores the power and place of the media in society. The cultural vocabulary used to structure the news is not simply a shared vocabulary; instead

the frame offers an encoded "preferred reading." Given possible multiple readings of mass media, the power of the news lies in its ability to ensure that readers or other active users are presented with the same or similar bureaucratically created and ideologically embedded accounts. Hence the frame may be more important than the specific details it organizes. (Tuchman 1983:335)

Again, journalists need to be understood to be active participants within social reality. They are not distanced messengers communicating observations in a particular tongue because it is understandable to the listener. Journalists are not simply providing an information service to a society of which they are not part. They are of society and they occupy an essential position within it.

The position of the press, and journalists' claims of objectivity and fairness, furnish the news media with extraordinary power. The media's claim to impartiality enables it to maintain its legitimacy. It is this claim, accepted by the public, which, to answer Weaver's question, gives the media the right to propagate their own distinctive vision. But it is not "their own" vision. It is a vision embedded in societal arrangements that reflect particular social interests. It is the appearance of impartiality—and indeed its approximate impartiality within the limits of conventional consideration—which is validated by, and serves to "validate the general framework of political discourse" (Bethell 1977:35).

News media that are impartial and fair are understood to present the world "the way it is." We then need not question the media's judgment of what is important and what is not, who is responsible and who is not, what is possible and realistic and what is not. Impartiality is the judge's robe that helps to dress the media in legitimacy and authority. It is impartiality that permits the news media to *shape* their accounts within preferred, ideologically embedded cultural stereotypes and thereby champion those stereotypes. (See Connell 1979 for a discussion of how television journalism accomplishes the work of "reproduction.") That is, it is by complying with society's sense of reasonableness and fairness that it upholds its privileged position to determine what is reasonable and fair. It is by being reasonable and fair that it can assume an "Olympian stance" (Bethell 1977:34) and maintain its power to promote particular social interests. "The power involved here is an ideological power: the power to signify events in a particular way" (Hall 1982:69).

COMPETING TRADITIONS OF MEDIA ANALYSIS

The understanding of the news media being suggested here is fundamentally different from that described in work within the tradition of administrative studies. The dominant paradigm for analysis has diverted attention from the ability of the media to define social and political reality (Gitlin 1978). It is specifically this power of the media and its contribution to the reproduction of existing social relationships that is a primary concern within the perspective suggested here. It will be helpful, at this point, to contrast the competing traditions of media analysis and more explicitly identify fundamental assumptions of each.

An immediate difficulty confronting an attempt to contrast competing perspectives is the determination of just how many perspectives to consider. Melody and Mansell (1983) and Blumler (1978), following the tradition of Lazarsfeld (1941), limit distinctions to "critical" and "administrative" research. McQuail (1985), in a review of the sociology of mass communication, contends that to identify only two traditions of research whether they be termed radical–functionalist, critical–administrative or Marxist–liberal/pluralist, is to ignore the fundamental split that exists between the "materialist wing" and the "more subjective variant" within the critical school. Fejes (1984) finds even greater distinctions within the critical perspective. Structuralists study the system and process of signification and representation as they analyze media texts. Political economists study the economic structure and process of media production, noting particularly the increasing monopolization and concentration within the media industry. The cultural studies strain of the critical perspective shares the concern of the structuralists about media message but understands the environment within which the message is produced and received to affect its content.

Curran et al. (1982) also see important differences within each of the major traditions. They identify at least four views of the media that have dominated its study since the period between the world wars. Initially, theories of mass society saw isolated anomic individuals as passive targets of the "word bullets" of brainwashing propaganda. This period was followed by a new "academic orthodoxy" that lasted from the late 1940s into the 1960s. This view, grounded in an assumption of political pluralism and supported by the findings of laboratory experimentation, saw a public selectively using and remembering communication and, therefore, a news media of only limited influence. By the late 1960s and into the 1970s earlier work was being reexamined more closely, and media effect was seen to depend on, among other things, audience attitudes and attentiveness, information sources, and the type of information involved. Finally, a Marxist theoretical perspective critical of the earlier empirical research tradition began to be established. This perspective saw media primarily as ideological agencies that maintain a system of class domination.

Bennett (1982b) also identifies four traditions of media theory, but for him the mass tradition begins in the mid-nineteenth century. Bennett next identifies the liberal/pluralist school and then cites the critical theory of the Frankfurt School, which attempts to incorporate mass society tradition into a Marxist framework. Most recent, Bennett suggests, is an effort by Marxists to develop a media theory within a general theory of ideology.

Clearly, the line between perspectives or traditions is drawn in accordance with a variety of criteria. These criteria are not always made explicit. Gitlin (1978) has identified three properties that characterize a distinctive paradigm. Any paradigm identifies important areas of investigation within its field, it makes use of a particular, more or less distinctive, methodology, and it produces a set of results that are recognized to be distinctive. A paradigm is determined not by specific procedures, but instead by consensus. Unfortunately, it appears difficult to establish or identify such a consensus. It seems that only in the most general way are we able to distinguish the fundamental qualities of competing alternatives. The identification of salient features depends upon the specific purposes for which we are making the distinctions.

Characterization of the fundamental differences between the critical and liberal/pluralist paradigms, for example, seems to be determined by the vantage point from which the differences are observed. The critical perspective is remarkable for its "orientation toward the question of power and epistemology," its redefinition of the question of causality and control of knowledge as the exercise of power (Slack and Allar 1983), or for its distortion through its "presentational organization of analysis" (Anderson and Sharrock 1979). It is unique in its recognition of the fundamental connection between media process and broader social and political relationships (Bennett 1982a), or by its refusal to subject its theory to "rigorous and wide-ranging empirical test" (Stevenson 1983). Work within the critical paradigm is distinguished by its rediscovery of the previously repressed issue of ideology (Hall 1982) or it is "intellectually self-limiting and sterile" (Lang and Lang 1983). The intent, methods, and contribution of the critical paradigm all seem to be issues of debate. While it does seem clear that there is a distinctive approach to the study of the media that is an alternative to "mainstream" studies, the characteristics and merit of the approach are contended. If we begin by considering some of the criticism directed against the critical approach followed by some self-description from within the paradigm, we might be able to identify the fundamental elements of both perspectives.

A Critique of the Critical Paradigm

One of the most forceful attacks on what they call media cultural studies is by Anderson and Sharrock (1979). Anderson and Sharrock claim that such studies assume their own reading of news accounts rather than the reading of consumers, fail to make the case that any bias they might identify is significant, and assert their own ideological concerns over the technical/professional issues faced by media producers. Radicals, according to Anderson and Sharrock, assert their claim of significant media bias through their play of "contrived surprise." By suggesting that the public expects media to be neutral, and then showing how media are in fact culturally biased, the critical theorists assume they have brought to light significant deceptive practices.

Anderson and Sharrock claim that anyone who has completed a first-year sociology course would not be surprised, but instead would recognize the necessity of such bias. The claim of media producers is of, and the expectation of the public is for, neutrality within the borders established by discussion among the major parliamentary parties.

There is no suggestion that atheists should be given equal time to match the output of religious broadcasting, the National Front, the Labour Party, or perverts, Mrs. Whitehouse. The television companies have open policies which relate television time to electoral popularity. Who in the world supposes otherwise? Who in the world supposes that where there are detectable minority positions against which "we" are united in disapproval, that the broadcaster is neutral? Assuredly, he is not.

Significant bias is not, then, to be found by identifying some under-represented viewpoint. Nor can it be established by reference to the validity and accuracy of what is reported since these are practical matters which are governed by, and are recognized to be governed by, limitations. . . . Only if we know what we have been promised shall we know if we have been deceived. (1979:368–69)

It is then only because media critics make unrealistic, indeed impossible, claims of what they—and the public—expect of the media, that they are able to suggest bias. The public, according to Anderson and Sharrock, have a better understanding of the media than do the radical critics, as the public recognizes the parameters of reasonable discussion and does not expect or want to hear the voices of those against whom they are united in disapproval.

The sources to which the media critics attribute bias, in the analysis of Anderson and Sharrock, are identified only through a most contrived and labored search. Rather than simply looking at the activities of journalists in their production of news,

The technique is to look "behind" the news into the bottomless pit of the world and its entire history, wandering across space and time until one falls upon an ideologically allowable cause. If, as is usual, that cause is far removed from its effect, then it does not need careful exposition beyond such amorphous characterization as "the cultural air we breathe," "society" or "capitalism." (1979:373)

It is then the ideological commitment or bias of the critic rather than that of the media that need be examined. Indeed, it is suggested that "one has to distort the things that the press and television say in order to commit the media to the kinds of 'theories' that sociologists sometimes claim are expressed by them" (1979:369). The problem is not with the media, but with the critics. "In much of the literature . . . it is not the details of media reportage which are in question, but the perceptual set which is adopted toward them" (1979:372).

A Critique of the Critique

Sharrock and Anderson's critique of radical media studies has itself been the object of criticism (see Murdock 1980). This criticism rests, in large part, on the claim that Sharrock and Anderson's reading of the literature has been selective, and this has led to its misrepresentation. It is apparent that Sharrock and Anderson identify a number of concerns that other critics too have directed toward "radical media/cultural studies." The problems asserted in these criticisms help us to understand fundamental assumptions of both those working within and those working outside the dominant paradigm. It has frequently been objected that the work within critical studies ignores findings that challenge its claims (for example, Altheide 1984) or even more commonly that the work is merely polemic as it makes no effort to subject its theory to empirical test (Stevenson 1983). Claims are implicit in Sharrock and Anderson's critique of critical studies that are themselves left unexamined and unquestioned except within the work that they criticize. Indeed, their assumptions, and those of the paradigm Sharrock and Anderson represent, form the basis of some of the most fundamental questions that motivate critical research. A uniform "we," united in disapproval of all that is not given consideration in the media, is required by a liberal/pluralist paradigm that understands the limits of consideration to be determined by popular demand. The media, in this view, are seen to be reflecting an achieved consensus that is not and need not be challenged. Such assumptions of the liberal/pluralist paradigm have, themselves, not been put to the test, within the theory but framed and underpinned it as a set of unexamined postulates. It should have asked, "Does pluralism work?" and "How does pluralism work?" Instead, it asserted, "Pluralism works"—and then went on to measure, precisely and empirically, just how well it was doing. This mixture of prophecy and hope, with brutal, hard-headed, behavioristic positivism provided a heady theoretical concoction which, for a long time, passed itself off as "pure science." (Hall 1982:59)

The claim of consensus serves to uphold the borders of reasonable and legitimate discussion featured in the media. The cloak of professed science defines the manner in which the media is to be studied and the concerns advanced in those studies.

In academic life, however, as in society more generally, an apparent consensus might conceal, but usually cannot bury, disparate visions. Challenges to the orthodoxy suggest that

the consensus question, in pluralist theory, was not so much wrong as incorrectly or inadequately posed. As is often the case in theoretical matters, a whole configuration of ideas can be revealed by taking an inadequate premise and showing the unexamined conditions on which it rested. The "break," therefore, occurred precisely at the point where theorists asked, "But who produces the consensus?" "In what interests does it function?" "On what conditions does it depend?" Here, the media and other signifying institutions come back into the question—no longer as the institutions which merely reflected and sustained the consensus, but as the institutions which helped to produce consensus and which manufactured consent. (Hall 1982:86)

Many of the questions about which critical researchers are most immediately concerned are the questions that liberal/pluralist researchers never ask. The matters these questions address are matters that form the foundation of unexamined assumptions of much of liberal/pluralist theory. It is particularly ironic then that much of the effort to denounce the critical perspective rests on the claim that the work within the paradigm is limited to ideological and theoretical posturing with little or no empirical test of its postulates. Stevenson suggests that debate between the competing traditions is fruitless and implies that the critical perspective can be discredited by simply "insisting on empirical verification, multiple operationalization, and the testing of necessary consequences of theoretical propositions. The natural sciences can serve as models and guide for a true science of human behavior" (1983:268). Hall's observations indicate that much of the work of the liberal/pluralist paradigm fails to meet Stevenson's own requirements.

Differences between the critical and liberal/pluralist perspectives (for purposes of discussion, thus far, it is sufficient to limit consideration to the two broad perspectives of media study) seem to be both theoretical and methodological. Theory of the critical perspective has directed its attention to matters not considered by the dominant paradigm, and the manner of investigation is frequently inconsistent with the demands of the model of science that directs much of liberal/pluralist work. The theoretical and methodological differences are related. They can be illustrated and better understood if we consider each perspective's treatment of the issue of "media effects."

Media Effects

Concern about the effects of the media on the public has characterized the behaviorist research tradition of media studies (Fejes 1984:220). The orthodoxies within the tradition have changed as research findings supported one or another assessment of effect, but the interest has continued. This has been accompanied by a relatively consistent conceptualization of what is meant by effect.

Until about 1940 the media was assumed to have a great deal of power to shape public opinion and belief (Blumler and Gurevitch 1982:240). Following World War II, work by or in the tradition of Lazarsfeld (Katz and Lazarsfeld 1955; Lazarsfeld and Kendall 1960) dominated the discipline. Such work focused on the specific measurable attitudinal and behavioral effects that media had on individuals who had been aggregated into categories determined by the purposes of the particular research effort (Gitlin 1978:207; Tuchman 1980:14). In a reexamination and summary of previous empirical research on effects, Klapper (1960) concluded that early work supporting the mass society thesis (that isolated and anomic individuals were highly susceptible to the media's influence) was a misinterpretation of the findings. Instead there are a variety of social factors that mediate between the media and the individual that serve to limit effect. Klapper's work, sponsored by CBS and supportive of nonregulation of the industry (Lang and Lang 1983:134), is a frequent citation in academic studies and the cornerstone of most "minimal effects" research.

Media effect studies, whether they found great effect as was common in the earlier studies or minimal effect as was common in later studies, shared an understanding of what it is they were looking for. They understood effect in a quite similar manner. Their research focused on individuals and small groups with the exclusion or lack of recognition of politico-economic contextual factors (Smythe 1984). The approach, consistent with the needs of positivist social science, assumed that the effects of media could be analyzed by the identification and measurement of changes in the behavior of individuals following exposure (Hall 1982).

The unit of influence is a short-term "attitude change" or a discrete behavior; or, more exactly, the report of such "change" or behavior by a respondent, and one which the respondent can attribute to some specific intervention from outside. (Gitlin 1978:214)

There is, in this conceptualization of effect, an assumed "commensurability of buying and politics" (Gitlin 1978:214). Lang and Lang, who see no reason why quantitative methodology cannot be used to provide an informed view of broader issues, agree that the social effect of the media was ignored in favor of a narrow concern for individual responses, as the latter was

a simple extension of the methods of marketing research to the study of media audiences. What publishers, public relations, and particularly broadcasters most needed was a measure of penetration—the rough equivalent of money receipts—to convince advertisers, educators, and every type of campaigner and protagonist that an investment in the communication they offered would yield returns. (1983:133)

Research motivated by such narrow considerations served commercial interest. But it seemed to inhibit analytic possibilities. Lasswell was able to characterize the study of communication as, "Who says what, in what channel, to whom and with what effect?" (quoted in McQuail 1985:94). Such a formulation, as McQuail notes, limits "attention to matters of avowed purposes, overt meaning, and communicative efficiency" (1985:94). A combination of the market concerns of commercial interests and a tradition of positivist social science in American academia together contributed to a study of the media conceived in very narrow terms of effects. (For discussions of the contrasting political/social and intellectual/academic origins of media research in Europe and the United States, see Bennett 1982b; Blumler and Gurevitch 1982; Carey 1983; Garnham 1983.)

More recently the theoretical foundations of studies of media effect have become more sophisticated. Fejes (1984) has summarized four models of effects that have placed the issue within a social or political context. Rather than defining the issue in terms originating in consensus or market penetration and commercial efficacy, these later efforts have identified the media as instruments for the distribution of information and knowledge and therefore as a source of power. "Agenda setting" theories understand the media to set the program of public discussion. It is the media that highlight issues and identify particular topics as social concerns. Until an issue is put into the public arena in this manner, it lacks the legitimacy of a concern recognized as shared and of importance throughout society. Once they are on the agenda and acknowledged by the media, issues are then more likely to be "noticed" by the public and to be understood to be significant enough to merit discussion. The "spiral of silence" is a variation or "negative mirror image" (Fejes 1984:225) of the agenda-setting model. Here, the ability of the media to keep issues from public discussion or to remove them from discussion is recognized. What we do not see as issues, what we do not discuss, is recognized to be as important as what we do discuss. Change in public opinion, in this view, rather than being an indication of persuasion or a conversion effect of the media, is the result instead of the spiral of silence having been broken. A new issue or perspective has penetrated the borders of public discussion. The "dependency model" of media effects might be understood to explain why we are reliant on the media to set the agenda of our public discussion. Individuals within a large and complex society do not have immediately available to them personal, first-hand familiarity with all that is going on within that society. We rely on the media to provide us with information about that of which we do not have immediate knowledge. More penetrating forms of this model note that the extent of our reliance on the media is influenced by the structure of the particular society and our place within that structure. The "knowledge-gap" model attends most directly to our relative positions in relationship to the media. Differential access to media and the information that it provides creates inequalities in informational resources. Resulting inequalities exaggerate those differences already existing, the knowledge gap therefore increases. Media then, in its unequal communication of knowledge, goes beyond maintaining social inequalities; it exaggerates them.

While these more recent theories are certainly improvements over earlier approaches to the study of media effect or media influence, they still suffer from some of the same difficulties. These models avoid, or even contest, the unquestioned political assumptions of pluralism but they still share the ontological assumptions that form the basis of a pluralist conception of power. They reflect the insights of power elite theories over pluralist theories but, like most power elite theory, depend upon the same fundamental vocabulary as the theory they attempt to refute. Pluralists and elitists argue over who has power in society. The discussion must be broadened to include a reconsideration of what we mean by power. If we are going to understand the significance of the media—or more fundamentally, if we are going to understand society—we must acknowledge, refine, and utilize alternative conceptualizations of power that provide the basis for more penetrating analysis.

Models of Power

As characterized by Dahl (1961), power in the pluralist model is distributed over a wide range of organizations with cross-cutting memberships. As issues of interest to particular individuals or organizations are brought into public debate, those involved mobilize their resources and form alliances with similarly interested others. Shifting alliances and cross-cutting memberships necessitate compromise and ensure that no particular interest comes to monopolize the decision-making procedure. There do exist competing interests in this model, but interests and power are diffused throughout a fluid arrangement of alliances where no particular interests prevail unchallenged.

The media, in the pluralist view, can be seen simply as a disinterested source of information where interested parties can obtain knowledge about the issues of contention. It can also be understood as a forum within which contending interests have equal opportunity to present their cases and mobilize the public to support their cause in a democratic decision-making process. While early studies suggested that monopolization and exploitation of the media would undermine the democratic process as individuals would be molded into the image preferred by exploiters, later studies, such as the work of Klapper, indicated that an individual's integration into various social groups moderated any possible effect of media exploitation. The effect—or power—of the media was then minimal. It would not interfere with democratic process as the understandings of individuals developed in their immediate social environment, among their friends and associates, resisted manipulation. The media was not the source of any great power and would not interfere with pluralist society. It would, in fact, be supportive of pluralism as it would provide the public with the information necessary for their purposeful participation in the decision-making process. The public was uniform in its identification with and influence within the democratic decision-making process, while, at the same time, varied in their endorsed outcomes. The media is here understood to be an institution central both to the necessary equalities and the informed differences required by pluralist democracy.

In his "three-dimensional" view of power, Lukes (1974) offers a provocative critique of the pluralist model. Pluralism, or what Lukes calls the one-dimensional view of power, is limited from the start by its ontological biases. Conflict, for the pluralist, is always observable. This "view of power involves a focus on *behavior* in the making of *decisions* on *issues* over which there is an observable *conflict* of (subjective) *interests*, seen as expressed policy preferences, revealed by political participation" (Lukes 1974:15). Pluralists refuse to consider that interests might be unarticulated or that people might even be mistaken or unaware of their own interests. By demanding that conflict must be directly observable, they have limited their understanding of interest, conflict, and power. It is this behavioral bias that shapes the conclusions reached within pluralist theory. Power, in this view, has little explanatory significance in the understanding of the development of consensus. If there is no conflict, the issue of power is irrelevant.

The study of media that simply provides information and identifies existing consensus need not consider the matter of power. Disagreement may exist concerning the selection of particular policy alternatives. Power will be exhibited in the formation of contending coalitions that will seek to determine outcome in accord with procedures to which both subscribe. Power then is seen in the coalition formation process and resulting activity, not in the identification of policy alternatives within the media or in the vocabulary used to define the world within which the contest takes place. Any media effect here would be discerned by identifying a change in the attitude of individuals toward one or the other alternative. Such an effect would be the result of exposure, through the media, to either otherwise unavailable information or the effective persuasive argument of one of the contending parties. The effect might be due to the biased presentation of the issues by the media, but this would be an unfortunate and inexcusable violation of journalistic responsibility. The analytic value of the concept of power seems limited to cases of its abuse, as in the isolated instances of the purposeful, biased presentation of reality. The proper management of the media involves the disinterested presentation of reality to the public.[3] Power involves purposeful behavior in the making of decisions on issues. The concept of power then is of no analytic value in the understanding of the media but in the exceptional case of the violation of journalistic ethics.

Thus, with an ontological bias that focuses on behavior and demands observable conflict, pluralists have eliminated the consideration of power from efforts to understand the routine or normal functioning of the media. Power is involved in decision making. Journalists do not make (political) decisions. Power is not a factor in journalistic activity. The strategic ritual described by Tuchman has been successful.

The later theories of agenda setting, the spiral of silence, the knowledge gap, and media dependence seem not only to make room for the consideration of power in the analysis of the media, but seem to be founded on the assumption that media institutions are instruments of power. These approaches originate in, or are at least consistent with, power elite theories. (See Dreier 1982 for an examination of the press's links to and place within the elite.) The power elite is a small portion of the population with similar self-interest and shared social experiences that form a relatively unified group as they pursue shared policy concerns. Their monopolization of power, based in their social or economic position, ensures that government decision making will serve their interest. The resolution of conflict within society will consistently favor the concerns of the elite as it is they who dominate the decision-making process.

Bachrach and Baratz (1962), building on the work of earlier power elite theorists (for example, Hunter 1953, who studied community power elite, and Mills 1956, who developed a model of the national power elite), have suggested that it is an error to limit a study of conflict and power to observable behavior, as an effective power elite can prevent important political issues from becoming public. Such suppressive efforts anticipate decisions that will provoke controversy and, in effect, create "non-decisions." Policies are determined without formalizing them as policies, decisions are made without public acknowledgment.

Lukes claims power elite theory, or the two-dimensional view of power, represents only a "qualified" critique of one-dimensional behaviorism (1974:20). The focus is still on active manipulation of events and observable, though possibly not obvious, conflict. Decisions, in this view, are still consciously and intentionally made. Elitists, like pluralists, adopt "too methodologically individualist a view of power . . . [they] follow in the steps of Max Weber for whom power was the probability of *individuals realizing their wills* despite the resistance of others" (1974:22). These approaches do not permit power to be sufficiently analyzed because they fail to consider how its effective administration is "a function of collective forces and social arrangements" (1974:12). The sociological study of power should not be limited to the examination of how individuals manipulate other individuals or their environment. Such study must instead acknowledge the social nature of power. Inactivity of leaders and the "sheer weight of institution" serve power relationships (1974:38). The very structure of social organization and the view of the world from within that organization can serve particular interests at the expense of others without the intentional, purposeful involvement of individual actors. No longer simply a resource possessed by some individuals or located within particular social roles, power is instead understood to be infused into the fabric of a social system.

Hegemony and Power

The three-dimensional view of power might best be understood by noting Lukes's debt to Gramsci (1971), and the complementarity between his conceptualization and Gramsci's "hegemony." Fundamental aspects of their analyses are similar, which enables each to be used with the other in the development of a fuller understanding of power and social relations.

Hegemony has been described as a world view "in which a certain way of life and thought is dominant, in which one concept of reality is diffused throughout society in all its institutional and private manifestations, informing with its spirit all taste, morality, customs, religious and political principles, and all social relations . . . " (Williams 1960:587; also see Boggs 1972; Williams 1973; Sallach 1974; and Patterson 1975 for discussions and refinements of the concept). As an "organizing principle" (Boggs 1972:92), hegemony structures our world view. Hegemonic ideology represents not simply a dominant view, but a world view that is seen as "natural." Our perceptions of the world and our ability to make sense of it or understand it are determined by, or at least shaped by, our vocabulary and our perceptual experiences. The tools we use to understand our world are provided for us within a social context. These tools serve to reinforce the stability of the social context. In this way the tools must be considered to be political in nature. Aspects of our life that are often considered nonpolitical, or civil, and independent of significance to the maintenance of state order, are, according to Gramsci, most important for an understanding of the apparent political consensus. Our socialization within a social order is not politically neutral but, instead, most fundamentally a political socialization (Miliband 1969).

In the "nonpolitical" arenas of our life we are introduced to images of great political significance. We experience impressions that shape our tastes, opinions, and attitudes. If hegemonic domination is successful those tastes, opinions and attitudes will serve to encourage political stability. Our experiences within the institutions of socialization will introduce us to manners of thinking, schools of thought, and general world views that are seen as natural—and, therefore, right. Hegemonic values and attitudes are inculcated by simple repetitive exposure, rather than considered judgment. Emotional relationships are established with ideals and values. We accept them on the basis of our emotional, almost visceral relationship with them. As politics is infused into our culture, a political ethnocentrism develops in the same manner as does cultural ethnocentrism. Alternatives will most often be discounted with little consideration. The alternatives lack legitimacy, not because they have been discredited after careful examination, but, instead, because they are immediately seen as meriting little examination at all.

Hegemony, then, becomes the "normal" form of control. Force and coercion, "militant" forms of control, need become dominant only in times of crisis. An effective hegemonic order creates a consensus that minimizes the need for coercion as it limits friction and antagonism. Enmity is minimized when the citizenry shares a common world view and sees its interests as basically complementary. Classes, though, do not share an identity of all interests. Recognition of some, though limited, conflict of interest is necessary to maintain the legitimacy of the hegemonic order. The conflict, however, is minimized and contained so as not to threaten the fundamental aspects of the social (class) relationships. The suggestion of compromise and sacrifice is made while hegemony ensures that what is essential is neither compromised nor sacrificed (Joll 1977:130). Gitlin (1980:256) has explained that

the hegemonic ideology of bourgeois culture is extremely complex and absorptive; only by absorbing and domesticating conflicting values, definitions of reality, and demands on it, in fact, does it remain hegemonic. In this way the hegemonic ideology of liberal, democratic capitalism is dramatically different from the ideologies of pre-capitalist societies and from the dominant ideology of authoritarian, socialist, or Fascist regimes. What permits it to absorb and domesticate criticism is not something accidental to liberal capitalist ideology, but rather its core.

Because liberal democratic capitalism is itself founded on conflicting and contradictory demands and values, in its hegemony we also find such contradictions. These are conflicts that must be absorbed if they are not to become challenges to hegemonic reality. Hegemonic ideology then, like the liberal capitalist state within which it exists, contains within it the potential source of its demise.

At the center of liberal capitalist ideology there coils a tension between the affirmation of patriarchal authority—currently enshrined in the national security State—and the affirmation of individual worth and self-determination. Bourgeois ideology in all its incarnations has been from the first a contradiction in terms, affirming the once revolutionary ideals of "life, liberty, and the pursuit of happiness," or "liberty, equality, and fraternity," as if these ideas were compatible, or even mutually dependent, at all times in all places. More recently, the dominant ideology has strained to enfold a second-generation set of contradictory values: liberty versus equality, democracy versus hierarchy, public rights versus property rights, rational claims to truth versus the arrogations of power. All opposition movements in bourgeois society—whether for liberation or for domination—wage their battles precisely in terms of liberty, equality or fraternity (or, more recently, sorority)—in behalf of one set of bourgeois values against another. They press on the dominant ideology in its own name. (Gitlin 1980:257)

As long as the contradictions are absorbed within hegemonic ideology, conflict is contained and social relations are preserved. It is an indication of the strength of hegemony that challenges are expressed in terms of hegemonic ideals. It is an indication of its vulnerability that conflicting hegemonic ideals become the rallying cry of oppositional forces within society. The balance of strength and vulnerability is in constant motion. It is the flexibility of hegemonic ideology that has enabled it to adjust to and absorb the conflicts that are most pressing at any historical period. It is this resiliency that has permitted bourgeois ideology to endure through "all its incarnations."

For Gramsci then, as with Lukes later, the existing social order contains within itself forces that do not require purposeful manipulation, yet serve to maintain the order with its dominant interests. If we are to understand the perpetuation of existing patterns of social arrangements, we cannot limit our focus to the intentional self-interested action of particular individuals or classes. If we are to understand the perpetuation of social arrangements we must recognize the power of those arrangements to perpetuate themselves. The most fundamental factor in the preservation of existing social relations is those social relations. Behaviorist social science, whether in the form of pluralist or power elite theory, does not permit the consideration of such a conceptualization of power. Pluralist and power elite theories then fail to appreciate the source and nature of the power of the media. Studies of gatekeepers, the social or political background of journalists (Johnstone et al. 1976) or even media ownership (Compaine 1980; Compaine et al. 1982), while somewhat informative, are—by their ontological assumptions, their conceptualization and operationalization of power—necessarily limited in the contribution they can make to the understanding of the social function and power of the media. In a similar manner, the media-effects studies mentioned above, by focusing narrowly on reportable attitude or behavior changes, fail to recognize and are unable to consider the most significant media "effect."

By posing power in terms of hegemony, attention in media study is redirected.

The concept of hegemony designates a model of power that revolves around the idea of social knowledge in the production of rule by consent . . . it focuses on the effectivity of communication in the maintenance of social control. The mass media, and the systems of representations that they produce, are analyzed for their effectivity in determining understandings of the social world. . . . The effectivity of communication is traced in the interaction of systems of representations and the negotiations over social meaning embedded in the practice of everyday life. (Slack and Allar 1983:216)

The concept of hegemony in critical media studies focuses consideration of the media not simply in terms of isolated problems, or institutions or practices (Carey 1983:313), but instead forces consideration of how the media shapes our knowledge of the world and how the media, as a source of knowledge, is a powerful force of social control.

Interpenetration of Social Institutions

Media effect (even the term is quite insufficient to convey the understanding of the role of the media in critical studies) is of a very different sort from that proposed in the behaviorist method of positivist science. The media are not isolated institutions that can be separated from the rest of the social landscape to be studied apart from the rest of the social environment. The forces that shape media organizations, as well as the force of those organizations, are part of a social totality. When we consider the meaning or power of the media within this totality, our concern is

no longer specific message-injunctions, by A to B, to do this or that; but a shaping of the whole ideological environment: a way of representing the order of things which endowed its limiting perspectives with that natural or divine inevitability which makes them appear universal, natural and coterminous with "reality" itself. (Hall 1982:65)

Media effect, or power, must not be "conceptualized in simple linear terms . . . power is exercised in and by social processes and institutions" (Slack and Allar 1983:215). Those processes and institutions, including the media, can only be understood in the context of the web of relationships within which they exist. In this way the divisions assumed between and among institutions, between social processes and institutions, between ideology and institutional structure or material base, even between media and social reality, are seen to be artificial and misleading. While such distinctions may be necessary for the purposes of communication, they frequently result in obfuscation.

The media must not be fully separated, even for analytic purposes, from other institutions of the social order. Depending on issues of concern, emphasis on particular aspects of the media's interpenetration with other institutions will be examined more or less closely, but the relationship of interpenetration must be recognized. To look at the media without acknowledging their relationship to and integration with the government, the economy, the institutions that train journalists, the readers and viewers and the rest of the complex of social forces, including cultural ideology, is to misrepresent and consequently to misunderstand them. Indeed, to isolate the "news media" from a more general consideration of the media, failing to recognize their entertainment function and economic requirements (concern for audience share, circulation numbers, consumer demographics, advertising income, and bottom line) is to also participate in artificial separation and to mislead. Investigation of any particular aspect of the media must acknowledge the fundamental nature of their integration within a particular social order.

Social processes within media organization, then, cannot be appreciated without consideration of the network of social forces within which organization participants and the organization itself are located. This is the sort of consideration made too infrequently by gatekeeper and social psychological studies. While what goes on within individual organizations and within the experience of individual journalists is important—both for what it tells us about individual cases and what it is able to tell us of a more general nature—the limitation of possibilities and experiences, again due to the location of the organization and individuals within a particular social order at a particular time, must be acknowledged. What is not, or cannot, be is fundamental to an understanding of what is.

A tension exists within media studies, indeed throughout all of social science, between the location of primacy in ideas and ideology or in structure and material conditions. When primacy is placed in one or the other location, it is assumed that society is ordered by a single set of dominant forces. To assume a choice must be made between ideas or material conditions is to assume that one can stand apart from the other and that their relative positions are constant, or nearly so, over time.

Neither can stand apart from, nor be reduced to, the other. Either ideas or material conditions may provide the dominant explanatory force at a particular time, or for a particular aspect of society. Neither can, at any time, stand alone either in fact or in explanation. Instead, each shapes, supports, and is supported by the other. Each can also be a source of the other's dissolution as conflicts and contradictions arise between the two elements or aspects (I hesitate to use the term "levels" for its obvious suggestion of priority) of society. Such conflicts and contradictions, as will be shown in the following case studies, can also originate within each of the societal aspects identified. Contradictions exist within both the structure and ideology of a social order. Conflicts between the two can highlight and bring attention to conflicts within each.

The suggestion that either structure or ideology can be reduced to or explained by the other, is subject to criticism similar to that directed toward behavioral conceptions of power. A single linear cause-and-effect relationship is assumed. Such an assumption precludes the possibility of a dialectical relationship of interpenetration characterized by mutual, variable, and unresolved influence. In short, it misrepresents the relationship by forcing it into a framework amenable to the requirements of positivist methodology.

Finally, and most fundamentally, the recognition that the media exist within an interpenetrated web of relationships that is the social totality demands acknowledgment of the impossibility of division between media and social reality. Again, the view of the media as a mirror of society, informing us by reflecting for us the parts of the world to which we are not directly exposed, assumes that the media, as well as its audience, stand or are at least capable of standing apart from what is reflected. Actually, the media resemble more than reflect. Media resemble the social reality of which they are part. They do so because they *are* part of that reality. Media institutions are part of what they report. The media are part of, elements in, society. It is one of the elements in a relationship of interpenetration with the other elements of society. In this way the media, like all other elements of the interpenetration, both shape and are shaped by, resemble and are capable of changing, the society of which they are part and the other elements of that society.

To understand the relative position or influence of the media at any particular time, we must examine the society and the media of that time. As in the previous divisions and separations, this one is artificial. Understanding requires that we recognize the parts of the social order in the interpenetrated context within which we find them. In this manner, all study of a social order, of society, must be ecological. Such study does not suggest "the substitution of multiple, interactive isolatable causes (as in regression analysis) for cause"; instead it is being suggested that elements, as aspects of society, "have no identity or effectivity outside of their interrelationship. The causal determinant is itself determined by the character of the interrelationship, not the sum of the individual elements" (Slack and Allar 1983:215).

It is the combination of work such as that of Gramsci and Lukes that provides the orientation for such an analysis. It is this orientation within which we can recognize and begin to understand the hegemonic frames that shape media presentation of news, how that presentation shapes our knowledge of the world, and how as a source of knowledge the media are a most powerful social force. The case studies that follow will begin to assist us in this effort. They will help us understand the nature of the media, while they will also contribute to the further development of the general theoretical orientation that guides the study.

NOTES

1. The example cited by Henry is an excellent one that actually illustrates more than Henry might like to acknowledge. At the end of the crisis, after the hostages were released, a news conference was held with the former hostages participating. Journalists' questions addressed issues of confinement and treatment of the hostages during their captivity. Toward the end of the conference a reporter took the microphone to ask the hostages to address the issues that led to the action of the Iranians and asked the hostages specifically for a comparison of their treatment to the treatment of Iranians by the U.S.-trained SAVAK. The reporter was unable to complete her question as other journalists present shouted and booed at her in an effort to drown her out. The press conference was soon terminated. The behavior of the journalists both prior to the questioner and in response to her is quite illustrative. The "crisis" was over. The hostages had been released. Yet the reporters' questions were still limited to those that indicate a very narrow "American" perspective. The issue for them was the hostages and their treatment by Moslem fundamental fanatics. There was little effort to understand the hostage-taking within a larger context—a context that would have provided a fuller meaning and understanding of the situation. It seemed not to occur to the reporters that there was a broader situation to consider. When someone (it would be interesting to be able to identify the questioner and her understanding of events) challenged the accepted definition of events, the reporters were not simply resistant but were intensely hostile. What codes or standards of appropriateness did the questioner violate? How do these codes and standards relate to the ideal of journalism? Journalists silencing a journalist: it is a powerful example of a shared commitment among journalists to a particular understanding of the world.

2. The effectiveness of this ritual, of course, can only be maintained if it is not recognized as a strategic ritual. Resistance to Tuchman's analysis, at least among journalists, was illustrated in a survey (Boyer 1981) of editors. The strongest responses regarding what was meant by objectivity were the negative reactions to the statement that objectivity is "A copout used by editors to avoid making decisions." Yet, the ritual does eliminate or at least significantly reduce consideration of many of the most fundamental journalistic issues, from what is news to what form the presentation of news will take.

3. Work in the tradition of White's (1950) gate-keeper study identifies management or organizational influences that shape news accounts, but in these studies power is still a measure of intentional influence that an individual has over the behavior of others. Little effort is made to place influential actors in a social position outside of the media organization or to identify common social qualities or characteristics of influential actors across organizations. There is little acknowledgment of history or the societal milieu within which these organizations are located. Such studies become the accumulation of accounts of individual anomalies in the otherwise pluralistic arrangement of power. The conceptualization of power is still limited to behaviorist operationalization. The focus on individual rather than societal factors is grounded in its general placement within American social science and its specific origin in Lewin's (for example, 1947) work with small groups.

REFERENCES

Altheide, David L. (1984) "Media Hegemony: A Failure of a Perspective," *Public Opinion Quarterly* 48:476–90.

Altschull, J. Herbert (1984) *Agents of Power: The Role of the News Media in Human Affairs* (White Plains, NY: Longman).

Anderson, Digby C., and W.W. Sharrock (1979) "Biassing the News: Technical Issues in 'Media Studies,' " *Sociology* 30:367–85.

Bachrach, Peter, and Morton S. Baratz (1962) "The Two Faces of Power," *American Political Science Review* 56:947–52.

Barthes, Roland (1973) *Mythologies* (London: Paladin).

Bartley, Robert L. (1981) "The News Business and Business News," in *What's News: The Media in American Society*, edited by Elie Abel (San Francisco, CA: Institute for Contemporary Studies), pp. 187–208.

Bennett, Tony (1982a) "Media, 'reality,' signification," in *Culture, Society and the Media*, edited by Michael Gurevitch, Tony Bennett, James Curran, and Janet Woollacott (London: Methuen), pp. 30–55.

——— (1982b) "Theories of the Media, Theories of Society," in *Culture, Society and the Media*, edited by Michael Gurevitch, Tony Bennett, James Curran, and Janet Woollacott (London: Methuen), pp. 30–55.

Bethell, Tom (1977) "The Myth of an Adversary Press," *Harpers* 254:33–40.

Blumler, Jay G. (1978) "The Social Purpose of Mass Communication Research: A Transatlantic Perspective," *Journalism Quarterly* 55:219–30.

Blumler, Jay G., and Michael Gurevitch (1982) "The Political Effects of Mass Communication," in *Culture, Society and the Media*, edited by Michael Gurevitch, Tony Bennett, James Curran, and Janet Woollacott (London: Methuen), pp. 236–67.

Boggs, Carl, Jr. (1972) "Gramsci's 'Prison Notebooks,'" *Socialist Revolution* 2:79–118.
Boyer, John H. (1981) "How Editors View Objectivity," *Journalism Quarterly* 58:24–28.
Breed, Walter (1955a) "Social Control in the Newsroom," *Social Forces* 33:326–35.
——— (1955b) "Newspaper 'Opinion Leaders' and Processes of Standardization," *Journalism Quarterly* 32:277–84.
Carey, James W. (1983) "The Origins of the Radical Discourse on Cultural Studies in the United States," *Journal of Communication* 33:311–13.
Charnley, Mitchell V. (1936) "Preliminary Notes on a Study of Newspaper Accuracy," *Journalism Quarterly* 13:394–401.
Coffey, Phillip (1975) "A Quantitative Measure of Bias in Reporting of Political News," *Journalism Quarterly* 52:551–53.
Compaine, Benjamin M. (1980) *The Newspaper Industry in the 1980s: An Assessment of Economics and Technology* (White Plains, NY: Knowledge Industry Publications).
——— (1982) *Who Owns the Media?* (White Plains, NY: Knowledge Industry Publications).
Connell, Ian (1979) "Television, News and the Social Contract," *Screen* 20:87–107.
Curran, James, Michael Gurevitch, and Janet Woollacott (1982) "The Study of the Media: Theoretical Approaches," in *Culture, Society and the Media*, edited by Michael Gurevitch, Tony Bennett, James Curran, and Janet Woollacott (London: Methuen), pp. 11–29.
Dahl, Robert A. (1961) *Who Governs?* (New Haven, CT: Yale University Press).
Dreier, Peter (1982) "The Position of the Press in the U.S. Power Structure," *Social Problems* 29:298–310.
Epstein, Edward Jay (1981) "The Selection of Reality," in *What's News: The Media in American Society*, edited by Elie Abel (San Francisco, CA: Institute for Contemporary Studies), pp. 119–32.
Fejes, Fred (1984) "Critical Mass Communication Research and Media Effects: The Problem of the Disappearing Audience," *Media, Culture and Society* 6:219–32.
Gans, Herbert J. (1972) "The Famine in American Mass Communication Research: Comments on Hirsch, Ischman and Gecas," *American Journal of Sociology* 77:219–32.
Garnham, Nicholas (1983) "Toward a Theory of Cultural Materialism," *Journal of Communication* 33:314–29.
Gitlin, Todd (1978) "Media Sociology: The Dominant Paradigm," *Theory and Society* 6:205–53.
——— (1980) *The Whole World is Watching* (Berkeley, CA: University of California Press).
Gramsci, Antonio (1971) *Selections From the Prison Notebooks* (New York: International Publications).
Hall, Stuart (1982) "The Rediscovery of Ideology: Return of the Repressed in Media Studies," in *Culture, Society and the Media*, edited by Michael Gurevitch, Tony Bennett, James Curran, and Janet Woollacott (London: Methuen), pp. 56–90.
Henry, William A., III (1981) "News as Entertainment: The Search for Dramatic Unity," in *What's News: The Media in American Society*, edited by Elie Abel (San Francisco, CA: Institute for Contemporary Studies), pp. 133–58.

Hofstetter, C. Richard (1976) *Bias in the News: Network Television News Coverage of the 1972 Election Campaign* (Columbus OH: Ohio State University Press).

Hunter, Floyd (1953) *Community Power Structure* (Chapel Hill, NC: University of North Carolina Press).

Johnstone, John W.C., Edward J. Slawski, and William W. Bowman (1976) *The News People: A Sociological Portrait of American Journalists and Their Work* (Urbana, IL: University of Illinois Press).

Joll, James (1977) *Antonio Gramsci* (New York: Penguin).

Katz, Elihu, and Paul F. Lazarsfeld (1955) *Personal Influence: The Part Played by People in the Flow of Mass Communications* (New York: The Free Press).

Keeley, Joseph (1971) *The Left-Leaning Antenna: Political Bias on Television* (New Rochelle, NY: Arlington House).

Klapper, Joseph (1960) *The Effects of Mass Communication* (Glencoe, IL: Free Press).

Lang, Kurt, and Gladys Engel Lang (1983) "The 'New' Rhetoric of Mass Communication Research: A Longer View," *Journal of Communication* 33:128–40.

Lazarsfeld, Paul F. (1941) "Remarks on Administrative and Critical Communications Research," *Studies in Philosophy and Social Science* 9:2–16.

Lazarsfeld, Paul F., and Patricia L. Kendall (1960) "The Communications Behavior of the Average American," in *Mass Communications*, edited by Wilber Schramm (Urbana IL: University of Illinois Press), pp. 425–37. Article originally published 1949.

Lewin, Kurt (1947) "Frontiers in Group Dynamics, Channels of Group Life, Serial Planning and Action Research," *Human Relations* 1:143–53.

Lukes, Steven (1974) *Power: A Radical View* (London: Macmillan).

McQuail, Denis (1985) "Sociology of Mass Communication," *Annual Review of Sociology* 11:93–111.

Melody, William H., and Robert E. Mansell (1983) "The Debate Over Critical vs. Administrative Research: Circularity or Challenge." *Journal of Communication* 33:103–16.

Meyer, Timothy (1972) "News Reporter Bias: A Case Study in Selective Perception," *Journal of Broadcasting* 16:195–203.

Miliband, Ralph (1969) *The State in Capitalist Society* (New York: Basic Books).

Mills, C. Wright (1956) *The Power Elite* (Oxford: Oxford University Press).

Murdock, Graham (1980) "Misrepresenting Media Sociology: A Reply to Anderson and Sharrock," *Sociology* 14:457–68.

Patterson, Tim (1975) "Notes on the Historical Application of Marxist Cultural Theory," *Science and Society* 39:257–91.

Russo, Frank D. (1971) "A Study of Bias in T.V. Coverage of the Vietnam War: 1969 and 1970," *Public Opinion Quarterly* 35:539–43.

Sallach, David L. (1974) "Class Domination and Ideological Hegemony," *Sociological Quarterly* 15:38–50.

Scanlon, T. Joseph (1972) "A New Approach to the Study of Newspaper Accuracy," *Journalism Quarterly* 49:587–90.

Schiller, Dan (1981) *Objectivity and the News: The Public and the Rise of Commercial Journalism* (Philadelphia, PA: University of Pennsylvania Press).

Schudson, Michael (1978) *Discovering the News: A Social History of American Newspapers* (New York: Basic Books).

Slack, Jennifer Daryl, and Martin Allar (1983) "The Political and Epistemological Constituents of Critical Communication Research," *Journal of Communication* 33:208–18.

Smythe, Dallas W. (1984) "New Directions for Critical Communications Research," *Media, Culture and Society* 6:205–17.

Stevenson, Robert L. (1983) "A Critical Look at Critical Analysis," *Journal of Communication* 33:262–69.

Stevenson, Robert L., and Mark T. Greene (1980) "A Reconstruction of Bias in the News," *Journalism Quarterly* 57:115–21.

Tuchman, Gaye (1972) "Objectivity as Strategic Ritual: An Examination of Newsmen's Notions of Objectivity," *American Journal of Sociology* 77:660–79.

——— (1980) "The Facts of the Moment: The Study of News," *Symbolic Interaction* 3:9–20.

——— (1983) "Consciousness Industries and the Production of Culture," *Journal of Communication* 33:330–41.

Weaver, Paul H. (1972) "Is Television News Biased?" *Public Interest* 26:57–74.

Westerstahl, Jorgen (1983) "Objective News Reporting," *Communication Research* 10:403–24.

White, David H. (1950) "The Gatekeeper: A Case Study in the Selection of News," *Journalism Quarterly* 27:283–90.

Williams, Gwyn A. (1960) "The Concept of 'Egomania' in the Thought of Antonio Gramsci: Some Notes on Interpretation," *Journal of the History of Ideas* 21:586–99.

Williams, Raymond (1973) "Base and Superstructure in Marxist Cultural Theory," *New Left Review* 82:3–16.

3

KAL 007

AN EVIL EMPIRE AND AN
INNOCENT PASSENGER FLIGHT

The news media that, according to the democratic assumption, are indispensable to the survival of democracy, are understood to be free and unfettered. Democracy requires, at minimum, the possibility of political pluralism that itself assumes equality of opportunity between and among contending parties. The development of a plurality of perspectives and the opportunity for equal expression of those perspectives demands a press that is accessible to and is a reflection of the multitude of potentially inconsonant voices. Such a press, with its variety of opinion and vision, makes possible the formulation of independent and unmanipulated views and understandings. A free market of ideas and values—a useful metaphor—is possible only when competitors have an opportunity for equal market participation, only when the media provide equal opportunity for expression. A free press makes available alternative understandings and provides the forum for competing perspectives. Such can be accomplished by either a press that provides expressive opportunity to all voices, or equally available presses for each voice. (See Schiller 1979, 1981 for a discussion of the change from advocacy journalism to the establishment of the commercial press and the concomitant development of concern about objectivity.)

A state-controlled press—usually assumed to be the antithesis of a free press—does not permit expression of competing voices. Neither does it permit the comparisons and critical evaluations that are necessary for the development and formulation of independent and unmanipulated understanding. A free press permits clarity of analysis and self-determination within and of a society. A controlled press fosters obfuscation and ignorance which permits domination. The objection to governmental—or any—control or manipulation of the media, for the democrat, originates not simply in disagreement with the views presented, but in the irresolvable conflict that exists between a bounded press and the requirements of democratic practice.

The bounds that inhibit journalistic process are not limited to those enforced by the strong arm of a government intent on maintaining an unchallenged position. The bounds of journalistic freedom can be influenced by forces more formidable, more deeply rooted and potentially more stable than specific individual political regimes. By comparing accounts within the American press, and by comparing accounts in this nation's press with those in the press of another nation, we might be able to identify what is particularly "American" about our own press. That is, we might be able to identify some of the specific bounds within which the free press of the United States functions. The purpose of the comparisons is to identify some of the assumptions that are basic to American political culture and thereby provide part of the ground upon which journalistic work, like all social activity, is accomplished.

The bounds maintained by our political culture, the unarticulated and unrecognized—or at least unquestioned—assumptions of what is natural, important, credible, reasonable, right or proper, can remain dominant, in part, because they are not experienced as being oppressive as they are not often recognized. We do not continually strain against the harness of hegemonic cultural assumptions because we do not feel constrained. Of course, there are times when we do experience the harness of our political culture, when our personal experience, or societal history, or other previously unquestioned assumptions conflict with that culture. The balance of cultural assumptions recognized and unrecognized varies with our history, both personal and social, but normalcy requires that the great core of assumptions unquestioned remains so.

Because we do not ordinarily recognize the bounds created by our political culture does not mean that those bounds do not interfere with democratic process. When the assumptions of our culture limit our social and political knowledge, or our choices, or when they can make possible either purposeful or systemic exploitation that benefits the particular interest of a minority, they violate democratic purpose. When those same assumptions shape media presentation, they can serve much the same function as the government of a controlled press. This is not to say that there are no differences between the free and the controlled press. It is instead to suggest that there are significant similarities. Each can serve to maintain nonreciprocal social and political relationships. As democracy requires at least political equality among individuals, any forces—experienced as oppressive or not—that foster inequality, also undermine democratic process.

A simple historical example can illustrate the force of assumptions of political culture in the inhibition of the practice of democracy. The original voting rights granted by our founding fathers were quite limited. It has only been through our history as the assumptions of our culture have changed, that franchise has been expanded to include an increasing number of citizens. We can now look back with offended sensibilities and acknowledge the violation of democratic ideals, but at the time the Constitution was written the strength of normative political assumptions denied most of the nation's population participation in what was considered a democratic political reality, despite the restricted political participation that precluded self-determination, fostered exploitation, and prevented the realization of democracy.

Current assumptions similarly limit such a realization. They shape our understanding of the world by placing blinders on us that permit only a very narrow vision. The world we see has limited possibilities outside of current reality. The blinders, held in place by the assumptions of our political culture, by hegemonic ideology, limit the visualization and hence the realization of alternative social realities while maintaining procedural democracy.

The narrowness of vision, or the strength of our hegemonic assumptions, can be examined by looking at accounts of the same incident from a variety of sources both within and outside of the United States. On the night of August 31, 1983, a Soviet fighter plane shot down a Korean Airlines flight en route from Anchorage, Alaska to Seoul, South Korea. A scrutinization of accounts of this event from selected news sources could illustrate significant differences and similarities that characterize the premises that shape those accounts. By looking at accounts within American news media, and then comparing those to accounts from the press of Canada, we can begin to recognize shared and divergent political suppositions that characterize the ideological hegemony of each society and filter their perceptions of the world. The assumptions or suppositions apparent in the reporting of the event will be shown to be significant as they are central to our understanding of the world.

The issues attendant to this examination of the news media are fundamental to our understanding of the process of political decision making. If our considerations in making such decisions, or in participating in the election of officials who make such decisions, are based on a foundation of unchallenged and—within a particular hegemonic order—unchallengeable assumptions, those considerations are, at least potentially, misguided and undemocratic. The fundamental purpose of this study then is to examine the notion of a free press upon which the democratic assumption rests. Democratic reality might require more of a press than that it be free from government manipulation. It might also require a press that permits penetration by counter-hegemonic realities.

THE NEWS MAGAZINES

Murder and Atrocity in the Sky

The cover stories of both *Time* and *Newsweek* the week of September 12 were about the Korean airliner. Responsibility and blame for the incident were communicated clearly and forcefully on the covers of both periodicals. Picturing an exploding Korean airliner with a Soviet plane in the foreground, the cover of *Time* was captioned "Shooting to Kill" and declared "The Soviets Destroy an Airliner." *Newsweek* pictured a gunsight superimposed over a Korean airliner pursued by a Soviet fighter plane on its cover. *Newsweek*'s cover was titled "Murder in the Air." The stories in the magazines were titled "Atrocity in the Skies" (*Time*, September 12:10) and "A Ruthless Ambush in the Sky" (*Newsweek*, September 12:16).

The covers and headlines reflected the content of the magazines' texts. While there might have been some specifics of the incident that were still unclear, enough was known to draw distressing but predictable conclusions. "Despite the many unanswered questions that continued to surround the incident, it was clear that the Soviet Union had committed a brutally provocative act, one that demanded an unambiguous U.S. response" (*Time*, September 12:11). The Korean airliner "had been cold-bloodedly blasted out of the skies"; it was "wantonly destroyed"; the incident was "a crime against all humanity" (*Time*, September 12:10). The incident served to substantiate the claims of Representative Lawrence P. McDonald, the chairman of the John Birch Society and a Congressman from Georgia who had been a passenger on the flight. "All of McDonald's political crusades . . . in the end came down to his bedrock belief that communism threatened to enslave the world. As he boarded Flight 007 for Seoul last week, McDonald could hardly have known how dramatically his world view would be played out" (*Newsweek*, September 12:27). This was not an isolated incident, but instead part of a continually unfolding scenario designed to enslave the world.

The incident was not only further evidence of the Soviets' grand design but also an indication of the methods by which they are attempting to realize their goals. The destruction of a passenger plane and the murder of 262 innocent passengers and crew "served as a telling demonstration of how the Soviet Union uses power." It "confirmed that Soviet commanders are always ready and willing to use force—when they can get away with it" (*Newsweek*, September 12:17). More than an indication, the incident is *confirmation* of what we already knew about the Soviets. *Time* quoted a "senior White House aide" as saying "It is further evidence that the President was right when he said the Soviet Union is a country that is essentially evil" (September 12:11). *Newsweek* did not feel the necessity to have an administration official speak for it. It closed its article about the incident by observing, "last week, over a barren Pacific island, the world witnessed the Soviet Union that Ronald Reagan had always warned against" (*Newsweek*, September 12:30). The action provided "a nasty self-portrait that shatters the reasonable image that the Soviets have been trying to project as part of their peace offensive to block deployment of U.S. Cruise and Pershing II missiles in Europe" (*Time*, September 12:18). The clear implication is that the missile buildup is necessary as the Soviets are anything but reasonable. No public relations effort on the part of the Kremlin can convince the world, against all the contrary evidence, that a Soviet peace offensive is sincere.

Normal Passenger Flight Somehow Gone Wrong

The murderous Soviet action indicated a structural inability within that society to make reasonable, responsible decisions. "It showed a bureaucratic decision-making process that could not distinguish between a military threat and an accidental civilian intrusion" (*Newsweek*, September 12:17). Clearly, for the news magazines, "There [was] no evidence that Korean Air Lines Flight 007 was anything but a normal passenger run that somehow went wrong" (*Newsweek*, September 12:17). What exactly had gone wrong seemed unclear but also relatively unimportant. It was the ultimate fate of the flight that was the object of attention and not how it arrived at its location when it met that fate. *Time* reported that the captain of the flight was unaware he was off course or that he had Soviet fighter jets trailing him. If he had known either, he would have notified Tokyo air controllers. Though he had contact with the controllers, his communications were only routine (September 12:14–17). Both *Newsweek* and *Time* noted that as Flight 007 was reporting its location in routine communication, Japanese radar was showing the airliner in Soviet territory (*Newsweek*, September 12:18; *Time*, September 12:14). *Newsweek* did acknowledge that "one mystery is why Japanese controllers apparently did not steer [Flight 007] back on course" (September 12:18).

A number of such mysteries are noted but never pursued in the news magazine accounts. Both ask directly how the plane could have strayed so far off course (*Newsweek*, September 12:18; *Time*, September 12:18). While it is possible the pilot, Captain Chen, purposefully attempted to fly a short-cut route in an effort to conserve fuel and thereby save the airline expense, "The South Koreans had reason to expect the worst from the Soviets" (*Newsweek*, September 12:18). In 1978 another Korean Air Lines passenger plane had been shot down over Soviet territory. Another possibility was some sort of mechanical failure of the navigational equipment. This, too, seemed unlikely as the plane, a Boeing 747, has three independent state-of-the-art navigational systems, and KAL flights near the Soviet Union carry additional navigational equipment. While it was possible ("a conceivable possibility"; *Time*, September 12:18) that there was a human programming error, it was unlikely since entry of data and coordinates into the computer requires a series of checks by at least three different crew members (*Newsweek*, September 12:18). *Newsweek* quoted a KAL spokesperson as acknowledging that "It is a very difficult thing for that aircraft to stray" (September 12:18). Despite the questions, the news magazines seem content to conclude "The full explanation [for the course deviation] almost surely will never be known" (*Time*, September 12:18).

Evidence of Soviet Responsibility

Enough was known, however, to conclude that the Soviet Union was responsible for "wanton slaughter in the skies" (*Newsweek*, September 12:16). *Newsweek* suggested that "the electronic evidence was convincing," the Soviets tracked the plane for two and a half hours (permitting the decision to shoot to be made at the highest level), the fighter actually trailed Flight 007 for 14 minutes before attacking, and the fighter had radioed to its ground control full recognition that it was a civilian commercial aircraft (September 12:16). As the facts are so clear, "Washington's most fitting response to the destruction of Flight 007 may be simply to play the tapes [of Soviet communications], and let the Soviets speak for themselves" (*Newsweek*, September 12:30).

Soviet communications, both between the interceptors and Soviet ground control and between the interceptors themselves, were understood to be clear evidence of Soviet malevolence. Tapes of parts of the conversation between the fighters and ground control released by the Reagan administration were interpreted by the administration and the press as indicating that the intruding flight was recognized to be a civilian airliner. Tapes and transcripts were further used to indicate that the fighter pilots made no effort to communicate with KAL 007 through internationally recognized procedures. In fact, "by some reports Captain Chen blinked his plane's navigational lights on and off, an international distress signal," suggesting it was Chen who attempted communication, and the Soviets ignored it. The account in *Newsweek* added, however, that in a radio communication with Tokyo, three minutes before the attack, the South Korean pilot mentioned nothing more urgent than to request a slight change in altitude" (September 12:20). *Time*'s reliance on administration transcripts of the tapes, and its attitude toward Soviet statements on the matter was clearly illustrated when responding to its own question of whether the intercepting fighters signaled the airliner and, if so, whether the crew ignored the signals. *Time* reported that the Soviets "of course" answered yes to both questions, but that the tapes do not support the claims (September 12:18). The standard of truth is the word of the U.S. government. We, of course, expect the Soviets to lie.

Soviet reticence, their reluctance to comment on the matter, and their unsatisfactory statements when they did comment, were understood as further evidence of guilt. Soviet leadership issued "sullen and specious responses to the unequivocal evidence of what had happened" (*Time*, September 12:10). Rather than being repentant for their murderous act, the Soviets issued only "an awkward nonapology" and "stilted regrets" (*Newsweek*, September 12:21, 17). Whether commenting or refusing comment, the Soviets seem to reinforce their media image. They either lie or fail to acknowledge the truth. Even their sympathies and regrets are not genuine, but instead are forced or manipulative.

Among the most blatant untruths by the Soviets was their claim that KAL 007 was part of an effort to gather intelligence information, that it was on a spy mission. While it was acknowledged in both news magazines (*Newsweek*, September 12:18; *Time*, September 12:14) that the area trespassed by the Korean airliner was among the most militarily sensitive in all of the Soviet Union (among other reasons for its extreme military significance is that it is the site of missile testing facilities and early warning radar systems), the claim that the civilian airliner was on an intelligence-gathering mission was presented as absurd. "Common sense . . . suggests that even the most expert observer flying some six miles high in the dim predawn light is not likely to see anything that U.S. surveillance satellites have not repeatedly scrutinized and photographed in far greater detail." To fail to appreciate this would be irrational. "But [on the night of August 31] rationality did not prevail" (*Time*, September 12:14).

The technical resources that the United States has directed toward this strategic area are considerable and impressive and would therefore make the use of a civilian airliner to gather intelligence quite unnecessary. The most sophisticated eavesdropping technology designed is directed to

pick up radar signals from Soviet ground installations and aircraft—tipping the United States to any Soviet alert in the area. Other receivers and antennas are then tuned to pick up radio transmissions between Soviet air-defense installations and interceptor aircraft. . . . Those conversations are then flashed to a unit of the National Security Agency, the supersecret government eavesdropping operation, for translation and analysis. (*Newsweek*, September 12:25)

The recent deployment of "a new satellite permits the flow of raw data in 'real time'—almost instantaneously—to NSA headquarters at Ft. Meade, Md." Simultaneously, the Japanese also monitor, translate, and analyze Soviet transmissions on their own (*Newsweek*, September 12:25). It was these monitoring capabilities that enabled interception of Soviet communications and acquisition of the tapes that the administration and the news magazines found so damning. With such resources, surely a civilian airliner is not a necessary addition to the security arsenal.

Previous Overflights

But these impressive resources, it was acknowledged, have caused some— including the Soviet Union—to ask why U.S. officials did not warn the airliner of its deviation from course. *Newsweek* assured the reader that

U.S. experts said the interception of signals around Japan is so wideranging and automated that there was a good chance no human ears were actually listening for much of the time, that the danger became apparent only in the final minutes of Flight 007—since other commercial planes have scrambled Soviet defense systems and flown on safely. (September 12:25)

This is a curious admission by the "experts"—KAL 007 and the 1978 KAL flight are apparently unique only in their end, not in their violation of Soviet airspace. The *Newsweek* report did not pursue this point, but both *Newsweek* (September 12:22) and *Time* (September 12:14)—in efforts to compare the Soviet action to response by the United States in similar circumstances—elaborate instances of Soviet violation of U.S. airspace. In the two years previous to the downing of KAL 007, the Soviet airline Aeroflot, which "has a habit of wandering over sensitive U.S. military facilities," did so 16 times. One "Soviet plane got 'lost' over Otis Air Force Base on Cape Cod. Another just happened to drift over Groton, Conn., at the precise moment when General Dynamics Corp.'s Electric Boat Division was launching the first Trident nuclear submarine." The account continued, "Soviet allies are prone to similar reconnaissance runs disguised as navigational errors. LOT Polish Airlines and CSA, the Czechoslovak airline, are notorious for their 'mistakes.' "

Time, too, noted that Aeroflot had been "a notorious offender" of off-bounds airspace in the U.S. It also mentions the two cases over New England as examples. Both flights, it notes, carried passengers "and possibly cameras or electronic eavesdropping equipment." It was reported that in the eight months prior to the KAL incident, 77 Soviet planes had entered U.S. Air Defense Identification Zones on the Atlantic Coast while on nonstop flights from the Soviet Union to Cuba.

Both magazines then note that it is not uncommon for East bloc airlines to violate U.S. airspace in an effort to acquire intelligence. The violations are reported by the airlines to be the result of navigational errors. The purpose of the "errors" is frequently "to pick up U.S. radar frequencies and record how long it takes for U.S. fighters to respond" (*Time*, September 12:14). While there was the reference in *Newsweek* to Western commercial flights entering Soviet defense systems, these overflights were not explained. According to *Time*, like the Soviets, Americans also send planes to violate airspace. "U.S. reconnaissance planes have done the same thing, near the U.S.S.R. border and have triggered the firing of more than 900 Soviet ground-to-air missiles, so far without a hit." The report added though, that for the Americans, "this aerial skirmishing seldom involves commercial aircraft" (September 12:14). Does this mean that commercial planes are used by U.S. intelligence forces? Is the difference between U.S. and Soviet use of commercial planes simply that the U.S. intelligence community uses them less frequently as it relies more on military aircraft? It seems from this admission in *Time* that commercial aircraft are only "seldom" involved in aerial skirmishes, and the quote of U.S. experts in *Newsweek* indicating that commercial planes had scrambled Soviet defense systems before, that the news magazines acknowledge the use of commercial flights in potentially dangerous provocations in Soviet airspace. Why then did the two magazines insist in both the tenor of their stories and in specific statements that KAL 007 was not, and in fact, could not have been, on an intelligence mission? Why did they steadfastly maintain that the Soviets wantonly destroyed the plane and committed cold-blooded murder when they themselves provide hints that commercial planes can and have been used to spy? While the magazines were claiming that simple common sense indicated that a commercial flight was incapable of obtaining any intelligence information that was not obtainable by more technologically sophisticated means, they also acknowledged that the administration would closely guard the "top-secret intelligence" that was gathered in the incident (*Newsweek*, September 12:25).

Contradictions and Inconsistencies

It is not simply a "double standard" that is indicated in the magazines. East bloc navigational "errors" were purposeful overflights intended to gather intelligence while Western navigational errors were truly innocent miscalculations, but the problem with reporting found here is potentially even more dangerous. The journalists seem to contradict and even deny their own reporting. The innocence of KAL 007 is a basic assumption of all reporting of the incident, yet the magazines' own stories indicate at least the possibility that the flight was not simply a passenger plane on an errant route. *Time* presented, in almost storybook fashion, the tale of the flight. It told of the experience of the passengers traveling to the Orient, the activities of the stewardesses, what meals would be served, what the fare had been for the passengers and what role family responsibilities or even chance seemed to play in the presence of some of the passengers on board. The human interest story of an innocent airline flight with personalized passengers was suddenly interrupted by an atrocity in the skies. The innocence of the passengers need not be questioned, but the innocence of the flight—despite the way the tale is told and because of some elements included in the tale—should be. The reporters' own stories seem to ignore and contradict important revelations that they have included. Noted but ignored and never considered were the history of commercial overflights by Western airlines, the intelligence-gathering potential of such flights that gather information about Soviet defense practices and capabilities by provoking a Soviet response that can be monitored by a network of electronic eavesdropping technology aimed at the area, and all the unanswered questions about how KAL 007 could possibly have gone so far off course and happened to wander over the most sensitive area of the Soviet Union on just the night that a missile test had been planned.

The issue here is not whether KAL 007 was part of an intelligence-gathering mission. The issue is instead, how, given the acknowledgment of the existence of information that, at the very least, suggests the possibility of intelligence involvement, the magazines absolutely deny that involvement. It will be suggested below that the presentation of news by the magazines illustrated here is an indication of both the degree to which a hegemonic view of the world has been internalized by journalists and the manner in which the seeds for a counter-hegemonic understanding of the world can penetrate the work of those same journalists. News media and the work of journalists, it will be shown, can at the same time be a force of hegemonic domination and potential liberation from that domination.

Sharing the President's Rage

The weeks following the issues of September 12, the news magazines continued reporting in much the same manner. The covers of the news magazines of September 19 read "Putting Moscow on the Defensive" (*Time*) and "Inquest on Flight 007" (*Newsweek*). Clarifying its cover, *Newsweek* headlined its story "Inquest on a Massacre" (September 19:18). *Time* headlined its story "Turning on the Heat," with a subhead of "The U.S. has Moscow on the defensive over the downed Korean airliner" (September 19:12). It seemed the magazines were themselves turning on the heat and joining the prosecution at the inquest. *Time*'s report of President Reagan's strategy following the incident also characterized the presentation and much of the imagery within the magazines.

The U.S., Reagan decided, would play the part of a prosecutor in the court of world opinion, presenting evidence of wanton Soviet destruction of civilian lives and demanding an accounting. . . . This way the dispute would be seen not as a superpower confrontation but as a conflict between the U.S.S.R. and the rest of the world. (September 19:13)

Clearly, the magazines identified with the President's efforts.

The Soviet attack on Flight 007 also gave the world an indelible lesson in the tactics and priorities of a police state. It offered the specter of a panicky Kremlin scrambling to somehow explain and justify the unconscionable. And it gave Ronald Reagan a fine opportunity to prove that the United States is different—and can show the way toward a saner conduct among nations. (*Newsweek*, September 19:22)

In an interesting acknowledgment *Newsweek* noted that in its effort to "stonewall" the Soviet Union was not entirely unique in the history of international relations.

Moscow was not the first government caught in a corner that it tried to lie its way out: humiliating echoes of the American U–2 incident or Watergate came to mind. But the body count of the 007 affair made the Soviet's shifting story especially offensive.

Apparently there are similarities but also significant differences in the extremes to which the Soviet and U.S. governments will go to maintain innocence.

The Soviets outdid themselves by charging that the United States was somehow to blame for the atrocity. After nearly seven decades of political cynicism and untrammeled power, the Soviet government easily believes that everyone behaves as it does. (September 19:36)

The Soviet's sole and complete responsibility for the incident were obvious. Their refusal to acknowledge culpability and their outlandish efforts to distort reality by claiming U.S. responsibility for the deaths of 269 innocent victims must only add to the world's condemnation of that society. Given the Soviets' act of wanton violence and their subsequent behavior, "all civilized people could back the president in denouncing a Soviet system that refused to even say it was sorry" (*Newsweek*, September 26:45). "In the act over the skies of the Pacific and in its reaction to it, Moscow almost compulsively undid itself" (*Time*, September 19:16).

When the Soviets did attempt to respond to questions about their actions, the magazines were hardly satisfied by the explanations offered. In an unprecedented news conference Marshall Nikolai Ogarkov, the Soviet Chief of Staff, attempted to offer a Soviet perspective of the incident. *Newsweek* reported:

Moscow finally did some explaining last week. But Ogarkov's rationale for destroying an unarmed passenger plane astray over Soviet airspace played too late and too lame to silence a building sense of global outrage. The message of a ruthless Soviet fighter killing 269 men, women and children had been bad enough. But the Kremlin only built on its blunder—lying for six days before conceding it had "terminated" Flight 007 because the plane had penetrated its "sacred borders." Then, instead of apology, Moscow blandly turned on the United States and said: "You're to blame."

Tangled in their own skein of excuses, half-truths and outright lies, the Russians managed to make themselves look as bad as Ronald Reagan had often painted them. (September 19:18)

Time also found Moscow's explanations incredible.

The Soviets switched their line from "Who me?" innocence to brazen defiance. Yes, said a statement by the official news agency TASS, the Soviets had "stopped" the flight. The reason, it said, was that although the plane was a civilian jet, it was on a spying mission for the U.S. That was a claim just about nobody outside the Communist world believed. (September 19:12)

At his news conference, Ogarkov suggested that Soviet ground controllers had confused KAL 007 with a U.S. reconnaissance plane that had been in the area. *Time* found this explanation "confusing" as Ogarkov also insisted that the Korean airliner was involved in a spy mission (September 19:16). *Newsweek* (September 19:19) explained that Ogarkov claimed that the reconnaissance plane and KAL 007 were part of a coordinated mission flying together until the KAL flight split off to enter Soviet territory. Once detected, the plane later identified as KAL 007 tried to evade intercepting Soviet fighters by changing direction, altitude and speed. Ogarkov expressed no doubt that Flight 007 was used as "an intelligence aircraft." The *Newsweek* account noted that Ogarkov's explanations contradicted the recorded conversations of the Soviet pilots on a number of issues. Again the tapes, or the administration's explanation of the content of the tapes, were seen as the authoritative material proof of Soviet guilt. Further, the reader was regularly reminded that a passenger plane would be too conspicuous if fitted as a spy plane, and still more importantly that "American satellites can take startlingly detailed photographs of any Soviet installation" (*Time*, September 26:21).

Acknowledging Unanswered Questions

Both *Newsweek* and *Time* acknowledged that there were many unanswered questions even in the Western accounts of what happened during the flight of KAL 007. In the September 19 issue of *Time* a bit more than two pages was spent "explaining the inexplicable" and trying to identify "[w]hat is known and unknown about the Soviet jet attack" (pp. 25–27). On the question of how the flight could have strayed so far off course, it is suggested that an erroneous entry of coordinates could be the cause. It was reported that after passing the fifth in a series of checkpoints "the plane appeared to head straight for Seoul." The suggestion was that it was after this point, over Neeva, that the crew mistakenly entered its destination rather than its intended route. While this suggestion should raise a number of additional subsequent questions, *Time* seems to imply that this is a plausible, if not likely, explanation. The article did not acknowledge any evidence that conflicted with the supposition that KAL 007 headed "straight for Seoul." *Newsweek*, in an account of how Soviet defense systems and fighter pilots had difficulty visually locating the KAL flight after it appeared on radar, reported that tracking systems followed its violation of Soviet airspace and its anticipated exit from Soviet territory. "Then, abruptly, it swung back over Soviet territory. This time the plane appeared headed for Sakhalin island, where the Soviets had even more sensitive military encampments" (September 19:24). Like most other evidence that is damaging to administration versions of events, this information was noted in passing, usually in reference to another point. But it clearly stated that rather than flying in an unvaried path across the Soviet island heading directly for Seoul (as would be necessary for the computer entry error explanation to be justified) KAL 007 changed direction during its flight. The change of direction brought it over areas recognized to be of particular strategic importance. Later in the account of events (p. 33) it was noted that by the time Soviet interceptors located the passenger plane, it "was once again on its way out of Soviet airspace." It is unclear from this account if another course change was necessary to head out of Soviet territory after flying over Sakhalin. This version of events is consistent with Soviet accounts and with accounts in *The Nation* that will be discussed below. Again though, the point of immediate concern is not to determine what "really" happened the night of August 31, but to examine media accounts of those events. Accounts in *Time* claim that KAL 007 flew a straight course, without deviation, to Seoul. This claim supports the suggestion that the overflight was due to navigational error but conflicts with evidence hidden in a *Newsweek* account, offered by Soviet accounts, and apparently available to *Time* journalists.

In response to the question of why Japanese or U.S. radar did not alert controllers and, in turn, Captain Chen, that KAL 007 was off course, the *Time* article suggested that the flight "fell between the cracks in the ground-control network." It was reported that the airliner was out of range of U.S. civil air control radar when it began to wander. While it was in voice contact with Tokyo, it was out of radar range. It was in range of Japanese Defense Agency radar but the JDA had no radio contact with the plane. Military radar records but does not necessarily track flights in the area, and does not routinely compare information with civilian controllers. Again, these explanations are inconsistent with information already provided by the news magazines. In explanation of why a passenger plane is not necessary to Western intelligence-gathering operations, readers had been told that sophisticated eavesdropping technology is directed to pick up radar signals from the Soviet forces that indicate any alert in the area. The deployment of a new satellite permitted the flow of data to National Security Administration headquarters in "real time." The Japanese also monitor the transmissions. The system was designed to monitor just the kind of defense activity that took place on August 31, yet the reader was told that the flight "fell between the cracks." As we will see below, procedures had already been established for contact between military and civilian authorities in such incidents involving civilian aircraft. The "between the cracks" explanation asks the reader to ignore the comprehensiveness and vigilance of an intelligence system with which the reader has just been impressed. One might have expected not only the reader but the journalists also to have difficulty reconciling the two explanations.

In the series of questions addressed in the *Time* article, it was acknowledged that even if incorrect coordinates had been entered into the computer of the Inertial Navigation System (INS) the crew would then have to subsequently violate a series of standard procedures and practices not to notice the mistake. Such disregard for what should be routine procedure would be difficult to understand on a flight that travels so close to a sensitive area. Similarly, suggestions that the crew might have chosen to try a short-cut route in an effort to save fuel could be discounted for the same reason. Not only would such a flight path take the airliner over Soviet airspace, it would then have to fly over North Korea. An American captain who flew the same route for 15 years was quoted as saying that "Not unless he was contemplating suicide" would the Korean captain attempt such a flight. *Time* added that

Because of their proximity to unfriendly skies, South Korean flyers are probably more sensitive about airspace violations than pilots anywhere else in the world. KAL Flight 007 Captain Chun Byung In, a retired Korean Air Force officer, was known as a cautious and skilled pilot. He was picked to fly for President Chun Doo Hwan on a tour of Southeast Asia in 1981.

Answering Unanswered Questions

The *Time* article next addressed the issue of whether the Soviets knew that the plane that they were firing on was a commercial passenger plane. It was asserted with certainty that the identity of the flight was known. "What is most clear from the incident is that the Soviets did not seem to care that their target was merely an innocent passenger plane." The plane could not have been confused with the U.S. reconnaissance plane RC–135 as the Soviets had suggested. Further, there was no evidence in the tape transcripts that the Soviet pilots made any effort to contact the Korean airliner to have it identify itself or warn it of its trespass. While the Soviets claim they fired tracer shots across the path of the intruding plane to communicate when other measures failed, *Time* reported "The transcript reports every action taken by each of the Soviet planes chasing the Korean airliner. There is no evidence that any warning shots were fired." In fact, there was no need for any warning at the time of the shooting because KAL 007 was only 11 or 12 miles from international air at that point and would be exiting Soviet territory in about 90 seconds.

Finally, *Time* again addressed the question, "Is there any basis to the Soviet contention that the Boeing 747 could have been used as a spy plane?" In answer, it was suggested that the plane does not have bays for photographic equipment or any electronic or communication devices necessary to gather intelligence.

Without extremely sophisticated equipment, which would require visible changes in the shape of the jet and the addition of large antennas, a high altitude flight at night by a 747 would have little use in reconnaissance. Such a mission would be worthless from a U.S. standpoint, since American satellites and the RC–135s provide for more detailed intelligence than any modified 747 could.

The conclusion is clear. In this article, and throughout the magazine accounts, though no explanation is suggested for how KAL 007 came to fly over two of the Soviet Union's most sensitive military and security areas, it was impossible that the overflight was an intended occurrence. It is outside the realm of possibility, given our culture and value of human life, that a U.S. administration, even in the interest of intelligence gathering, would risk innocent lives. In further evidence reference was continually made to the availability of other intelligence-gathering resources. In contrast, the accounts consistently assume the worst motivation and intention of the Soviets. While Americans have a supreme respect for human life, Soviet actions were explained in terms of a disregard for life and a readiness to murder and wanton destruction.

It was impossible that Western planes could be fitted with surveillance equipment, yet navigational "errors" by passenger flights of East bloc nations were designed to bring specially equipped planes over important U.S. military locations. The possibility that the KAL flight served an intelligence-gathering purpose not in the surveillance capabilities it itself possessed, but instead in the opportunity it provided for other intelligence sources to monitor the responses it provoked from Soviet defenses was not acknowledged by the news magazines, even though it was reported that Eastern passenger flights "wander" for just that reason and that Western military flights serve the same function.

While it may not be possible to suggest with certainty that the flight of KAL 007 was intended to be a central element in an intelligence-gathering mission or even that once it inexplicably began to wander, intelligence services exploited the development for its potential informational value rather than taking steps to correct the course of events, these scenarios, when they were acknowledged at all, were dismissed out of hand as not simply improbable, but instead as impossible. Absolute reliance on American good will and unquestioning acceptance of government-supplied transcripts of taped Soviet communications make such dismissal possible. It is the definitions of the nature and intentions of the East and West, specifically the Soviet Union and the United States, that are central to our political culture—our common understanding of the social/political world—that promote the assumptions of America's good intentions, our trust in our government, and our suspicion of and antipathy toward the Soviets.

The strength of these assumptions is indicated in the response of the news magazines to revisions by the administration of its own story. It was reported in the September 19 issue of *Newsweek* that it had

learned that U.S. officials now believe that the Soviets did at first confuse KAL 007 with a U.S. RC–135. Although the officials still maintain that the Soviet pilot who shot down the plane knew it was a commercial airliner, the transcripts of his cockpit talk suggest that he did not say anything to his commanders. (p. 22)

The suggestion seems to be that the pilot willfully led his commanders to misbelieve the identity of the intruding plane by not sharing his knowledge with them. It was not indicated how officials determined that the pilot knew the plane he was tracking was a commercial flight. Further, this suggestion seems quite at odds with the next suggestion that the pilot strictly followed procedure and that the destruction of KAL 007 was an example of the consequences of the rigidity of the Soviet system.

The following week *Time* (September 26:21) observed, "Despite the wealth of transcripts released by Japan and the U.S., there were still doubts expressed about the U.S. version of the incident, even among Americans." The nature of those doubts, as indicated by a *New York Times*/CBS News poll referred to in the article, seems quite interesting. While 61 percent of the sample suspected that the government was "holding back information that the people ought to know," 56 percent felt that the administration's actions in response to the Soviet attack had "not [been] tough enough." Apparently the suspicion was that the information being withheld by the administration would only show the Soviets to be more culpable and dangerous than already suspected. When there is confusion or incomplete knowledge, the ambiguity is resolved by the force of preconceived notions and expectations provided by our conception of the world.

The following, from the *Time* account, gives further indication of the character and strength of those notions and expectations. It was explained,

The U.S. added to the confusion by revising its transcript of the radio transmissions of the Soviet pilots who pursued Flight 007. The amended version was the result of an electronic enhancement of the tapes, which is standard procedure in such a case. It was immediately publicized by the State Department, even though it somewhat undercut the American position. A remark by the pilot of the Su–15 that shot down the airliner, originally said to be unintelligible, was revised to read, "I am firing cannon bursts." This seems to buttress the Soviet claim that its pilot had fired tracer shots to warn the Korean jetliner away from Soviet airspace. (September 26:22)

If the report had ended at this point the impression would be of a possibly paranoid but not necessarily evil Soviet empire and a well-intentioned and forthright U.S. government. Then government, when it acquired additional information—even though potentially damaging to its absolute damnation of the Soviet Union—shared it with the public. (The suspicions of the respondents to the *New York Times*/CBS poll would obviously be unfounded.) The report continued. Apparently, the new information was not necessarily damaging to the U.S. position after all. The reader was told next that there was "no indication" of whether the cannons had been fired in warning or as part of the attack on the passenger flight. Cannons on Soviet intercepter jets, it was reported, do not usually carry tracer ammunition. In any case, it was concluded, even if tracer shots were fired, it does not matter as the Korean pilot did not notice them. (In *Newsweek*, September 26:42, it was acknowledged that the question about whether the cannons were fired as a warning or in attack was the suggestion of "U.S. officials.") In what had originally appeared to be a report of evidence that would undermine at least some part of the administration's account, we find by its end, not only indication that the administration was voluntarily forthcoming—it is honest and can (should?) be trusted—but also that the new information does not really damage the account anyway.

More than a month and a half after the destruction of KAL 007 a one-column story titled "Second Opinion" appeared in *Time* (October 17:25). The story carried the subhead "What did the Soviets know?" In what initially appeared, again, to be a report of findings that fundamentally damaged both the credibility of the U.S. government and its specific, central claim of Soviet willingness and intention to murder innocent civilians aboard a commercial passenger airliner, we find instead a reaffirmation of Soviet culpability that is based on the analysis and assertion of the U.S. government. On the issue of the administration's claim of "irrefutable" proof that the Soviets knew KAL 007 was a passenger jet, *Time* reported that

last week the Administration admitted that the proof, far from being irrefutable, was nonexistent. Said State Department Spokesman Alan Romberg: "We do not have evidence" to show conclusively that the pilots of the Soviet interceptors and their ground controllers knew what kind of plane they were downing.

Romberg was responding to reports in the *New York Times* that most U.S. intelligence experts believed that the Soviets mistook the passenger flight for an RC–135. *Time* reported that it had learned from intelligence officials that the most that could be said was that there was no evidence that a positive identification was made one way or another. That is, the Soviets were not certain what it was they were shooting at. The magazine then suggested that there are obvious physical differences between a 747 and an RC–135 and that, whatever the case, the attack was "utterly inexcusable." The article concluded with a quote from Romberg. Referring to the Soviets, he asserted, "They had the responsibility to find out. If they didn't, they were incompetent or negligent or both." It appears that the "second opinion" referred to in the article's headline was little more than the slightest modification of the original opinion. In *Time*'s explanation of the "inexplicable" in its September 19 issue, it was asserted that "What is most clear from the incident is that the Soviets did not seem to care that their target was merely an innocent passenger plane." While the "most clear" aspect of an "inexplicable" incident had become clouded, the conclusions did not seem to have changed. It was without an acknowledgment of irony that *Time* relied on a spokesperson for the administration, which had claimed irrefutable proof for its reaffirmation of the assertion of Soviet culpability. It seems as unlikely, regardless of any evidence, that the U.S. government and its position would be significantly challenged as it is that any ambiguity would be added to the view of the Soviets as evil incompetents.

THE *NEW YORK TIMES*

In examining the coverage in *Time* and *Newsweek* of the events and issues surrounding the Soviet attack on KAL Flight 007, we have basically followed the chronology of the presentation. Doing so has permitted themes or frames to become apparent. Suggestions have been made about the assumptions that are the origins of those themes. Consideration of coverage presented in a daily newspaper would permit a more detailed examination of how themes are presented and developed. An examination of the coverage of the KAL 007 incident in the *New York Times*, paying particularly close attention to the themes identified in the newsweeklies, can, in addition to improving our understanding of the character of a "newspaper of record," also potentially better inform us of both the origins and consequences of the use of specific frames common in the media.

Before examining the reports in the *Times*, it will be instructive to note specific issues surrounding the KAL 007 incident and identify their importance in a determination of the meaning and significance of the incident. A most basic issue or question concerns how the Korean airliner got so far off course and came to fly over such sensitive Soviet territory. The official U.S. story claims that the flight strayed innocently from its intended course. The Soviet interpretation of events claims that the overflight was intentional and calculated, part of a coordinated spy mission. The way in which the *Times* deals with this issue could tell us much about the world assumed by its journalists. The second potentially telling issue is whether or not Western ground controllers or radar operators knew the flight was off course and, if they did, whether they then communicated, or were able to communicate that information to appropriate authorities. Information about these questions might indicate whether the overflight was intentional, or, if it was accidental, whether there was a willingness on the part of U.S. authorities to exploit the situation for potential intelligence gains. Finally, there are the possibly related issues of whether the Soviets attempted to communicate with the Korean airliner and whether they had identified the plane as a civilian flight. Clarification of these matters could help understanding of the incident as an issue of national defense or one of human rights. The Soviets defined the shooting as the former while the U.S. administration defined it as the latter and as an indication of the Soviets' attitude toward life and innocence. It will be instructive to examine how the *Times* treats these issues.

Veering Off Course

In its initial report about the missing Korean airliner it was explained in the *Times* that while the plane might have been forced to land on Soviet territory, its "loss" was also possible (*NYT*, September 1:1). It was reported, "There is speculation that the airliner might have veered off course while flying near Sakhalin, whose southernmost tip is 25 miles from Japanese territory." This initial statement of the situation is important because it provides some early, immediate definitions of the incident and, consequently, provides the first impressions of the affair for the reader. It is therefore important to try to understand the meaning of the account. First, it is not clear whether the speculation about the flight having veered off course referred to the possible location of the plane or to how it arrived at its location. The *Times*' account includes an Associated Press report that the Japanese Air Force tracked the plane flying near Sakhalin Island. After one or more other planes were observed flying close by, the Korean plane disappeared from the radar screen. It was known then that the plane was off course; there need be little speculation about its location. The reported speculation must then have referred to how it had arrived at its location. The presentation in the *Times* makes it seem possible, if not likely, that the plane simply "veered" mistakenly off course. After all, the southernmost tip of the island over which it was flying is only 25 miles from Japanese territory. A miscalculation of 25 miles from course on a flight of thousands of miles does not seem mysterious or untoward. But the deviation from course was hundreds of miles, not 25. The original flight plan would have taken the airliner on a path quite distant from the edge of Japanese and Soviet territory. The information that one point on the island of Sakhalin is 25 miles from Japanese territory is superfluous and potentially or even necessarily misleading. Again, the impression left the reader in this initial account was of an unfortunate but understandable course deviation.

The importance of this impression becomes more apparent when we look at the next day's reporting.

The page 1 headline on the following day read: "U.S. Says Soviet Downed Korean Airliner; 269 Lost; Reagan Denounces 'Wanton' Act" (*NYT*, September 2:1). It was reported:

There were no known survivors of the attack, in which a heat-seeking missile was said to have been fired without warning at the airliner by an interceptor that had tracked it over Soviet territory for two and a half hours.

It would seem from these accounts, so far, that a civilian airliner had innocently deviated slightly from course; it was followed for two and a half hours by an armed Soviet plane that suddenly, without warning, fired a sophisticated missile at the airliner, destroying it and murdering its passengers. Such Soviet action could certainly be termed "wanton." Two days later, on the first page of the *Week in Review* section of the Sunday edition of the *Times*, in an article not labeled "opinion" or "analysis," Leslie H. Gelb reported:

Ever so rarely, something happens that cuts through the ambiguities of politics and proves a point. Last week, a Soviet fighter plane shot down a South Korean passenger airliner that had strayed over Soviet territory, killing 269 people. The point, if it needed affirmation, was that the leadership of the Soviet Union is different—call it tougher, more brutal or even uncivilized—than most of the rest of the world. President Reagan said the incident was "horrifying" and cause for "revulsion," whatever the exact or possibly extenuating circumstances.

The Soviet invasion of Afghanistan and its intimidation of Poland may be explained away, at least in part, as power politics. But not this and not acts such as trumping up charges against dissidents, not inhuman and elemental acts, to judge by the reaction of Congress and elsewhere....

In the short run, the incident lends great weight to Mr. Reagan's portrayal of the Soviet Union as an "evil empire." (*NYT*, September 4:D1)

The events of the night of August 31, and the interpretation of those events, at this point, seem free from any ambiguity or uncertainty. However, a closer examination of reports in the *Times* indicates the events of the night were not known with certainty or clearly understood, and that the *Times* itself acknowledged the uncertainties and ambiguities, though the acknowledgment was often submerged under dominant themes such as those indicated in the Gelb quote.

On the issue of how the KAL flight could have strayed so far off course, there seemed to be no satisfactory explanation. It was reported that officials of the airline "contended that the airliner could not have strayed off course into Soviet airspace because of what they called 'sophisticated' navigational equipment on board" (*NYT*, September 2:4). According to this report and others (for example, *NYT*, September 3:6) the plane, because of its route, carried more navigational equipment than is standard on 747s. In addition to multiple computerized navigational systems, the plane's technology also included radar equipment that enabled the crew to follow coastline and other terrain features. Further, "the crew would normally have been able to verify the proper functioning of navigation systems . . . when their Boeing 747 jumbo jet flew past a powerful radio fix at the end of the Aleutian Island chain." It was reported that the "availability of such electronic aids only magnified the puzzlement among safety experts as to why the South Korean crew deviated from course and strayed deep into Soviet territory" (*NYT*, September 3:6).

Over the next days and months a variety of suggestions were made about how the flight could have come so far off course. One suggestion was that the deviation from flight plan was purposeful as it was an attempt to take a "short cut" in an effort to save fuel. U.S. intelligence analysts, it was reported, had said that "they could not rule out the possibility that the Korean crew might have flown intentionally into Soviet airspace on a short-cut route to Seoul" (*NYT*, September 4:18). The course that the plane seemed to be flying was the shortest route to Seoul, and an intelligence official was quoted as having observed that the plane had been on the wrong path for several hours, never deviating from the path that would have taken it straight to Seoul. (As has been noted, and will be discussed again below, the plane did not follow a straight, unvarying flight path. But in the first days following the incident this was not reported or acknowledged by official sources.) The article later acknowledged that intelligence officials had reported that to intentionally fly through Soviet airspace would be "unthinkable" to experienced pilots. It was suggested, however, "that other explanations, such as faulty navigational equipment were even more unlikely." Despite these acknowledgments, more than a week later the *Times* was still reporting that there was speculation that the crew might have intentionally flown into Soviet airspace to save fuel (September 13:11). The headline of this September 13 article, "South Korean Airline and Its Pilots Have Reputation for Being Aggressive," seemed to reinforce the speculation, but later in the text it was noted that other pilots considered it "inconceivable" that Soviet territory would be intentionally violated. One "longtime American pilot" was quoted as saying:

As individuals, some of the Koreans are tough, hard-edged characters. That's the reason they have had a reputation with some people for being kind of macho pilots. But to suggest that the Korean pilots take risks with passengers' lives is unfair and untrue.

Another suggested explanation for how the Korean Airlines flight could have flown so far off course assumed that the crew released the plane from computer control (to go around a cloud or thunderstorm) and neglected to put it back. Without navigational checks, provided by either the crew or the computer, the plane would have flown for hours in the wrong direction (*NYT*, September 11:16). Support for this theory, too, rested on reports that the plane had flown in a straight line with no course adjustments or changes.

A third reported explanation, one that seems most frequently cited and one reported to be supported by international investigation, suggested that the plane's course resulted from the misentry of coordinates into an onboard computer. It was reported (*NYT*, September 4:19) that the Japanese Defense Agency had suggested that the crew might have mistaken latitude for longitude when they entered flight coordinates into the navigational computer. In his final message to Japanese controllers, the last digits of the latitude and longitude reported by Captain Chen were the opposite of those of his actual location. Some days later (*NYT*, September 9:11) it was again reported that there was speculation that navigational coordinates had been improperly entered. The article suggested that even this explanation can be found wanting. If the data entry error had been made in Anchorage, "there are several checkpoints after Anchorage, and the pilot would have had to punch in the wrong numbers each time." Further, it was reported by another Korean pilot (Kim Chang Kya, the pilot of a flight in 1978 that had been forced to land in the Soviet Union) that it was standard procedure for other crew members to check the numbers entered each time. He was quoted as saying, "A mistake like that is very hard to imagine." He suggested further, "Everybody uses weather radar in that area" due to the sensitivity of the area.

Indeed, just two days after the first report of the incident, an article in the *Times* (September 3:6) had suggested the unlikelihood of such a data entry error. There were three computer navigational systems. They were "completely independent of each other, in order to provide back-up and check each other." It was reported, "It is possible to make a mistake.... But the numbers can be read on an electronic display.... And it was standard practice for one crew member to check on the entries of a colleague." It was further noted that there were nine checkpoints along the designed route. Each of the checkpoints can be entered into the computer before the flight, and "air traffic rules require that pilots report to traffic control centers when passing over six of the nine way points...." Later articles (for example, *NYT*, September 20:19) confirm that the starting point and nine subsequent check points along the route are routinely entered into the computer system prior to take-off.

These earlier articles then would have made it difficult to anticipate the headline two months later that read, "Computer Input Error Suspected in Korean Airliner's Bad Course" (*NYT*, November 17:10). Written by Richard Witkin, the same journalist who wrote the September 9 and September 20 articles, this article reported that the current theory to explain the KAL 007 flight path "is that a one-digit 300-mile human error was made in putting the take-off location into onboard computers." While Witkin notes a number of warnings that the crew could have noticed to recognize that the flight was off course, he concludes his article with a quote from an official of the International Civic Aviation Organization. The official suggested, "Whatever scenario you try, you have to make the assumption the crew weren't paying much attention. They'd flown R20 [the designation for the intended route] so many times, they probably treated it like a milk run." Less than a month later (December 8:9) Witkin reported the conclusions of the ICAO's investigation into the incident. The organization's report suggested one of either of two possible human errors, either a computer input error or the misuse of automatic pilot, was the cause of the course deviation. The report concluded, "Each of these postulates assumed a considerable degree of lack of alertness and attentiveness on the part of the entire flight crew but not to a degree that was unknown in international civilian aviation."

Below, it will be noted that there are a number of possible problematic aspects to the ICAO report, most important of which is its reliance on information provided by official Western sources and their refusal to consider information at odds with their (admittedly) tentative conclusions. A more immediate issue is the nature of the *Times*' reporting on the issue of the cause of 007's flight path. The newspaper's own early reporting provided information that undermined the credibility of its own later accounts and the conclusions of the investigating organization. It seems that as time went on the newspaper abandoned or disregarded information that it had itself provided the public. This is most startling when we attend to bylines and recognize that individual journalists who wrote the initial accounts also wrote the subsequent stories. How, if the flight had three independent navigational computers, if the crew would have had to enter wrong numbers at each of the checkpoints on its flight, if it is standard procedure for the crew to check on each other's data entries, if the crew had reported their passage over the series of checkpoints as required by air traffic rules, if "everybody" uses weather radar in the area, how, given all this previously reported in the *Times*, could it be concluded that crew inattentiveness explained how such a flight path could have occurred? At the very least, the conjoining of a series of most unlikely probabilities would be necessary to permit such inattentiveness and the consequent flight path. The scenario would require, in addition to the simultaneous inattention of the entire crew for a period of hours, the repeated entry of specific wrong numbers into each of the computers, the simultaneous malfunction of at least two and possibly all three of the computers, the incompetence of the crew in their identification of location at each checkpoint, and the incompetence of controllers who apparently did not question any of the reports of the crew. As it is from information provided in accounts in the *Times* that questions arise regarding the strength of the inattentiveness explanation, one might wonder why the journalists who wrote the stories and others who are responsible for and shape the newspaper seem not to address serious questions to the proposed explanation. As we will see immediately below, the matter of how Flight 007 strayed is not the only aspect of the *Times*' coverage of the flight that contains information that seems to undermine the frames used in the presentation of the story.

Who Knew and When Did They Know?

In addition to the question of how the Korean Airlines flight came to be so far off course is the question of who, if anybody, knew, during the flight that the plane was not on its scheduled path. Initial accounts in the *Times* reported that the last contact between civilian Japanese air controllers and Flight 007 occurred at 3:23 a.m. (September 1:D19). The same article includes the observations that the plane disappeared from radar six minutes after the last radio contact and that, according to an Associated Press report, the Japanese Air Force had not been able to pick up the airliner on its radar at its reported location. A few days later (*NYT*, September 4:18) it was reported that intelligence experts were examining tapes of conversations between Flight 007 and Japanese air controllers and between Soviet interceptor pilots and their ground commander in an effort to determine more specifically what happened the night of the shooting. It was noted in this article that "American officials have said that the United States had no ability to monitor the conversations as they were taking place or to warn the plane that it was in jeopardy."

The following day it was reported (September 5:1) that a U.S. spy plane had been in the same area as the Korean airliner. Reports by both the Associated Press and United Press International quoted administration sources as saying that the U.S. RC–135 and the KAL flight had at one time been within 75 miles of each other. However, it was noted in the article that the planes were last in the same vicinity two hours before the Korean plane was shot down and that by the time of the shooting the RC–135 was more than 1,000 miles from the scene. While note of the distance of the RC–135 from the scene of the shooting was apparently intended to indicate the unlikelihood that the Soviets mistook the civilian plane for a military spy plane, the article noted that "the disclosure of a second plane in the general vicinity of the Korean jetliner . . . raised new questions about an already confusing episode."

Among the confusing issues regarding the episode are the matters of U.S. monitoring capabilities and the role of the RC–135 in those capabilities. It was reported in an article headlined "U.S. Intelligence Plane was on a Routine Mission,"

Intelligence experts out of the Government . . . said that if the surveillance plane was operating anywhere near the path of the South Korean plane during the early phases of its encounter with Soviet aircraft, the American plane would likely have detected unusual Soviet air-defense activity. If so, they said, the crew of the plane could have taken steps to notify civilian air-traffic controllers in Japan. (*NYT*, September 5:4)

The primary mission of the RC–135 fleet, according to the *Times*, "is to track Soviet air-defense activity and missile tests." The article noted that

The planes, which are operated by the Air Force primarily for the National Security Agency, collect information about the abilities of Soviet radar systems, monitor communications between Soviet jet fighter pilots and ground controllers and observe the final stages of test flights of Soviet intercontinental ballistic missiles.

The information presented in this article seems to conflict with the claims of U.S. officials reported earlier that the United States had the ability neither to monitor the conversations as they were taking place, nor to warn the crew of 007 of their peril. Why is an article containing so much information that is potentially damaging to the administration's presentation of events under a headline presenting the administration's position? The *Times* maintained its frames or themes of presentation even as it provided information that threatened those themes.

Clearly, most accounts in the newspaper support rather than undermine the frames of presentation. Most frequently, conflicting information is identified deep within stories, not in the headlines or first paragraphs. Interestingly, though, sometimes it is the headlines and early paragraphs of stories that can alert a careful reader to the existence of alternative views. The day after the information about the purpose and capabilities of the RC–135 was presented, a front-page headline declared "President Says Spy Jet Landed Before Incident" (*NYT*, September 6:1). Among the points noted in the article was that the RC–135 had landed an hour before the Korean airliner was shot down, that both aircraft had been in international airspace when they were closest to each other, and that the monitoring equipment on the spy plane was directed to missile communications rather than to air defense transmissions. These points are responses to matters raised outside officialdom, and, for the most part, below the headlines and lead paragraphs. But an attentive reader might recognize, in the almost "out of context" nature of the information, a cue to read for a subtext.

The account of the presentation of Japan's representative to the United Nations was made in a similarly unintentionally informative manner. Headlined, "Japan's Civil Radar Too Far Away to Pick Up 747," the first paragraph of the article reported that the Japanese civil radar installation closest to where the Korean plane was shot down did not have sufficient "range to pick up the plane on its radar scopes" (*NYT*, September 8:11). Japanese traffic controllers "were consequently in no position to spot the plane's deviation from its assigned course or to warn the crew that the plane had strayed into Soviet airspace." While military radar tracked the Korean plane for 17 minutes, they were unaware that it was a civilian airliner. The article then suggests that while

[t]here were still some gaps in the information available to aviation and other officials trying to reconstruct events . . . the Japanese statement to the United Nations appeared to go a good way toward answering Soviet questions as to why efforts had not been made to establish contact with the airliner and guide it away from Soviet airspace.

In this case, it was acknowledged in the article that questions had been raised about Western accounts of events. The questions are attributed solely to the Soviets, which reduces the legitimacy of those questions. The *Times* further has made a judgment regarding the satisfactory nature of the Japanese response to the issues raised. The Soviet Union, as will be indicated below, was apparently not satisfied with the response, as Soviet officials and media continued to charge that the incursion was an informed, intentional act.

The *Times*' evaluation of the Japanese statement, in addition to being different from that of the Soviets, seems to avoid consideration of information that had been provided on the pages of the newspaper in earlier days. As noted above, on September 1, the *Times* reported that Flight 007 disappeared from radar six minutes after its last communication with Japanese ground controllers. It is possible that the reference was to air force radar and not civilian radar, though that is not clear. What is clear, however, is that the Japanese Air Force did not locate the flight at its reported coordinates. The air force then was aware that a civilian airliner was not on its scheduled course. However, they were (according to *NYT*, September 8:11) tracking an unidentified plane in Soviet territory for at least 17 minutes. Is it unreasonable to expect interest to have been piqued or suspicions raised among the military at the coincidence of these two developments? If such an expectation is not unreasonable, then does the fact that civilian radar could not track the Korean plane go "a good way" in explaining the lack of warning to the plane? The reader knows—if the Japanese Air Force had been unable to locate 007 at its reported location—that civilian and military controllers and radar operators are in communication with each other. The lack of civilian radar capability explains little, given the capability of military radar and the additional capability of communications between civilian and military controllers. Further, the treatment of the issue in the *Times* did not consider the role of U.S. ground controllers, radar, and intelligence technology. The newspaper some days earlier (September 5) had reported to readers the detection and communication capabilities of U.S. intelligence and a few days later was to report that Japan participates "in a global surveillance network directed by the Defense Department, the Central Intelligence Agency and, in particular, the National Security Agency, the nation's largest and most secretive intelligence organization" (*NYT*, September 11:D2). Again, even limiting consideration to factors identified in reports of the *Times*, it seems there was still quite a way to go to explain why efforts had not been made to warn the Korean airliner. Such an explanation might exist, but if that explanation is to be convincing, it must address the issues raised, but not pursued, in the *Times*.

Two weeks after the original incident, the *Times* carried a headline that initially appeared to undermine administration claims that it had no knowledge of the Korean airliner's flight path and the subsequent Soviet response as it was occurring. But the subhead and the content of the article proved to support official versions of the matter. A story headlined "U.S. Had Noticed Activity by Soviet" appeared on page 12 of the *Times* (September 14:12). The subhead read, "But Spy Agencies Assert They Didn't Realize Airliner Was Reason for the Moves." The story reported that U.S. intelligence detected air defense activity by the Soviet defense forces in the region prior to the attack on Flight 007. The activity was thought to be part of an exercise. Intelligence indicated that a Soviet surface-to-air missile unit on Kamchatka has been ordered to track a target that was identified as a U.S. RC-135. It was explained that because the Americans had no such plane in the area, little was made of the communication. Further, it was suggested, even if it had been known that the Soviets were responding to a civilian plane, there was no established procedure for linking U.S. intelligence with civilian aviation authorities.

This article is interesting for a number of reasons. It is both exceptional and routine at the same time. It is exceptional, of course, in its provocative headline. It is routine in the manner in which it immediately dismisses the apparent implications of the headline. It is routine also in how it ignores or fails to account for information within the article, or presented earlier, that is inconsistent with its theme and conclusions. It is frightening to imagine that the intelligence forces maintaining U.S. security are unable to distinguish between a Soviet exercise and an actual Soviet attack.

This inability, however, was not seen to merit the attention of journalists at the *Times*, except as it provides an explanation that seems to absolve U.S. forces of any responsibility in the incident. It was reported that even if intelligence authorities had recognized the gravity of the situation, they would have been unable to communicate with civilian authorities. This suggestion contradicts common-sense expectations and both previous and subsequent reports in the *Times*. Readers already knew that Japanese military authorities and civilian aviation officials communicated. Were U.S. security and intelligence agencies less competently designed? Further, if Japanese military and civilian officials communicated, and the reader had been informed that the Japanese intelligence system was integrated into and supervised by U.S. intelligence, it would not seem to have been impossible to pass communication through the Japanese Air Force to civilian air controllers in this dangerous situation. Reporting in the *Times* does not consider any of these possibilities. Despite its own presentation of information that suggests questions with regard to official statements of events, those questions were not pursued but instead only occasionally and perfunctorily noted.

Had questions been pursued in the *Times* reports, suspicion regarding official claims about the limitations of military/civilian communication would have been fueled less than a week after the article about the Soviet "exercise." The reliability of official claims that there were no procedures to link military and civilian air authorities was undermined by comments by the head of the Federal Aviation Administration, J. Lynn Helms (*NYT*, September 19:7). According to Helms, there were established communication links between military and civilian radar sites. The links could be used in a routine situation to report a straying plane. Helms added that military tracking capabilities might not be available to back up the civilian system if the military was already preoccupied with its own mission. Helms' statements appeared not in an article examining the earlier claims of communication procedures, but instead in an article documenting the inability of U.S. authorities to monitor the flight of the Korean passenger jet. The article was headlined "FAA Chief Says Jet Was Beyond U.S. Radar." (This claim, too, as was indicated in an article that was to appear in *The Nation*, August 18/25, 1984, is not free from critical review.) No mention was made in this article of how Helms' acknowledgment of military-civilian communication links directly contradicted repeated earlier denials of such links by official sources. Consideration of such contradictions might have served to undermine the credibility of the official government story. This aspect of the FAA administrators' comments was not pursued—or, we can surmise, even recognized. Instead, the important contribution of Helms' comments was identified as his confirmation that the Korean plane was beyond the range of all U.S. radar at the time it strayed and that the United States is therefore absolved of any responsibility in the incident.

The basic trust of journalists in government officials, their assumption that official accounts of this matter reflect fundamental truths and that the administration was as forthcoming as possible given the reality of national security concerns, was illustrated again when it was reported that the State Department was preparing a "white paper" that would provide "as much detail as is available on the shooting down of the plane" (*NYT*, September 18:1). The implication is that the State Department, representing the government, will compile, organize and share with the public all the information that it possesses. The inconsistencies, contradictions and incompleteness of previous government statements, all included—though infrequently fully attended to—in *Times* accounts, apparently had not dampened journalistic trust in officialdom.

Resolving Contradictions

This trust is all the more interesting when it is noted that the journalists did recognize the incomplete and sometimes confusing nature of official accounts. From the beginning, it was acknowledged that the Soviet attack on the Korean passenger jet "occurred amid several puzzling circumstances" (*NYT*, September 2:1). It was noted that "Amid conflicting reports and in the absence of many specific details about what happened, there were numerous unanswered questions" (*NYT*, September 2:4). During the next month, articles of various lengths appeared in the *Times* with the headlines, "Unanswered Questions" (September 2:4); "Some of the Things That Don't Add Up About Airliner" (September 4:18); "Points of Contradiction on Airliner" (September 7:16); "Korean Jetliner: What Is Known and What Isn't" (September 8:1); "Principal Points in Dispute Between Soviet and the U.S." (September 10:1); and "Korean Jet: Points Still to Be Settled" (September 26:6).

It seems that it was in articles such as these that treatment of the issues was most even-handed. Even here, though, there was a pattern of treatment that illustrates the common assumptions of Soviet liability and U.S. innocence. In the article identifying those things about the incident that "don't add up," for example, after enumerating a number of issues, it was suggested that

The hardest questions and those least likely to be answered are about the Soviet plane: Did the Russians know that the Korean airliner was a passenger air flight? Did they, as the Soviet Union says, try to warn it before shooting?

It was acknowledged that "There are also some questions on the American side." But these questions do not address the issue of possible U.S. responsibility in the incident. Together, the Japanese and U.S. governments possessed tapes of the conversations between the Soviet interceptor pilots and their commanders and Flight 007 and air controllers. The questions addressed to the U.S. side were primarily concerned with the release of those tapes to the public. The questions directed toward the Soviets then had to do with their culpability, while those directed toward the United States had to do with evidence of the Soviets' culpability. The reader was told that there was good reason for the Americans not to release the damning evidence. The article concluded with the explanation that was provided by a spokesperson for the administration. "A White House spokesman said the transcripts were held until President Reagan made a decision about them and related matters. He added that the administration wanted to release the transcripts in a suitable forum."

While some of the important and fundamental questions were sometimes raised, their significance would not be identified or pursued. Early in the article identifying what was known and what wasn't, for example, it was suggested, "Although American officials have pieced together much of what happened to Flight 007 over East Asia, there are still these questions." The theme of the article then is of questions that still remain, even while U.S. officials are trying to reconstruct events of which they had no immediate direct knowledge or participation. When the first question is then listed (Why was the airliner in Soviet airspace—"Was it an accident or was it deliberate?") the message is, if it was deliberate the U.S. government must have played no part. If it had, it would not then have had to "piece together" what had happened. Similarly, the next questions listed: Did controllers or intelligence know it was off course? And what did controllers do when they determined the jetliner was missing? are either to be directed toward the Japanese or not to be taken seriously. Again, if U.S. intelligence knew the plane was off course U.S. officials would have less to piece together as they would have been aware of events as they were developing. Further, if it was known that the plane was off course and was not aware of its location, additional questions would then be raised about why the pilot had not been informed of his peril. The rest of the unknowns listed in the article included whether the Soviet pilot who had made visual contact with the plane failed to identify it as a commercial flight, who issued the order to shoot the plane down, whether Captain Chen of Flight 007 issued a distress signal, and, finally, why KAL officials had been led to to believe that the plane had landed safely on Sakhalin Island. This last issue noted is interesting and not often noted. Airline officials first told families of passengers that the flight had been forced to land in Soviet territory but that it was a safe landing. It was not until hours later that the families were informed of what really happened. Korean officials claim they received all information about the flight from intelligence services of the United States and Japan.

Possibly the most interesting in the series of articles is one that appeared toward the end of September, written by Leslie H. Gelb, the journalist who four days after the downing of the Korean plane identified the incident as one of those rare events that cuts through the ambiguities of politics and proves a point. The article identified a number of issues that still required settlement. The first matter considered addressed the issue of why neither the United States nor Japan—the two nations responsible for air traffic control—knew the passenger jet had entered Soviet airspace. While Gelb noted that the claim of U.S. officials that they knew nothing of the disaster until after it had occurred had not been disproved, he added, "Given the variety of tracking abilities available, however, this seems somewhat surprising." While officials within the government had claimed that even military radar did not have sufficient range to have followed the flight, Gelb noted that former intelligence officials maintained that the U.S. military had over-the-horizon radar and radio navigational ability to track most planes around the globe. Additionally, Japanese radar, he noted, feeds into the U.S. system; the administration acknowledged being aware of increased Soviet surveillance and Japanese officials had both radar and communication contact with the Korean flight. It appears that Gelb might have become aware of more ambiguity in the incident than he originally recognized.

In addressing the issue of how Flight 007 could have come so far off course, Gelb noted that in the past five years there had been four cases of incorrect data in three independent computers that had caused navigational difficulties on other flights. He concluded that the deviation of flight path could have been due to computer error or crew incompetence, or it could have been a deliberate path in an effort to take a short cut. On whether the path could have been planned as part of a spy mission, as the Soviets maintained, Gelb suggested that he found "The consensus of current and former intelligence is no. Nonetheless, Congressional committees have begun full-scale inquiries." While during the 1950s U.S. passenger planes on their way to Berlin were used to spy on East Germany, there is little other history of use of commercial flights to spy for U.S. intelligence agencies. Use of Flight 007 in a spy mission, according to Gelb, would add nothing to U.S. intelligence- gathering capability and would not provide any new information. Gelb did add though, "There have been rumors over the years of ties between Korean Air Lines and the CIA, but no proof."

On whether the Soviets had grounds for thinking that the flight was engaged in a spy mission, Gelb acknowledged that the Korean plane did fly over the most sensitive of regions and that an RC–135 had been close to the passenger plane. Soviet officers, he observed, are "not trained to give the benefit of the doubt." On whether the Soviets were able to identify the intruding flight as a commercial plane, Gelb again presents alternatives but concludes the alternative most damaging to the Soviet case. While the interceptor was apparently close enough to make an identification of the plane, he was below the airliner so he was unable to see the distinguishing hump of the 747. But Gelb concludes, "Even if the hump is not seen, the 747 is almost twice the size of an RC–135." Clearly, the pilots should have been able to recognize the passenger jet. If it had been known that the plane was a commercial flight, would the Soviets have acted any differently? Gelb observed that Soviet officials had declared the shooting a proper action whether the flight was civilian or military. However, in the next sentence he acknowledged that most recently "low-level Soviet spokesmen have said the incident involving Flight 007 was a 'mistake,' with one official saying it was a result of a 'trigger-happy' pilot."

Gelb's work here is exceptional in a number of respects. The tenor of the article is obviously quite different from that of his September 4 article. It also acknowledges issues ignored or even denied in other accounts. His consideration of information regarding U.S. tracking abilities is particularly noteworthy. But he fails to follow through on his observations and identify their significance. What difference does it make if the plane had been tracked by U.S. officials? What does this possibly suggest about the officials or about the flight? If, as Gelb suggests, there could not have been any intelligence function to the flight, how might he explain the failure of radar operators and intelligence officials to warn Captain Chen? Gelb's conclusions seem to be limited by his original assumptions. A primary assumption, maintained despite evidence that he and a few others cite, is that government officials are being forthright and frank.

Part of the reason for the confusion surrounding the incident, according to Gelb, was that "The Reagan administration decided to issue a definitive statement right after the incident and before all the information it possessed had been processed." It is the premature release of administration statements that is a problem, not the withholding or manipulation and distortion of information and the distribution of misinformation. Admittedly, "The Americans are withholding some information," but this is "possibly to avoid compromising intelligence procedures."

Did Soviets Warn 007?

Two issues that must to be examined if the shooting of the Korean airliner is to be understood are whether the Soviets attempted to communicate with or warn the crew of KAL 007 of their peril and whether the Soviets knew the plane was a commercial flight. While the matters are related, each can provide information of a slightly different sort. Information regarding possible communication and warnings can help us understand Soviet procedures and policies and possibly the intent of the Korean crew. Information about Soviet identification of the plane, on the other hand, can tell us much about Soviet intent and mentality. The significance of these issues, in turn, makes the journalistic treatment of the issues central to an effort to understand news presentation.

The transcript of a news conference with Secretary of State George Shultz quoted him as responding to a question about whether the Soviets had warned the crew of the airliner by saying, "We have no information about that . . . as far as we can see there was no communication between the two aircraft . . ." (*NYT*, September 2:5). In an article on the same page on which the transcript appeared, it was noted that "One American official said the Soviet planes tried to get the Korean airliner to land and decided to shoot it down when that failed." This official's comment was reported in the twentieth paragraph of a 34-paragraph article about Shultz's news conference and the State Department's view of the incident. Despite the apparent contradiction between Shultz's statement and that of the unnamed official, it was reported that "Mr. Shultz and Mr. Burt [Richard Burt, the Assistant Secretary of State for European Affairs] gave unusually detailed descriptions of the events of the last 24 hours." This assessment was provided despite evidence, provided within the article, that Shultz, in his news conference, had provided at least misleading and incomplete information or had, more accurately, prevaricated. Again, as noted above, journalists seem to have assumed a forthright, open, and forthcoming character of government officials despite the inclusion, in their own accounts, of evidence of the contrary.

The seeming unquestioned acceptance of official accounts was again illustrated the following day (September 3:6). The first paragraphs of a story headlined "Korean Jet Signaled Russians, U.S. Says" reported that the

South Korean airliner tried to signal it would comply with established interception procedures before it was reportedly shot down in the Sea of Japan by a Soviet jet fighter on Thursday, senior American intelligence officials said today.

The officials said a preliminary analysis of communication between Soviet pilots and ground commanders indicated that the pilots of the Korean Boeing 747 . . . were aware of pursuit by Soviet aircraft and following procedures to signal that they were prepared to comply with instructions from the Soviet planes.

The claims that the crew of Flight 007 was aware that they were being pursued and further that it communicated to the Soviet pilots that they intended to comply with Soviet instructions is inconsistent with, or even directly conflicts with, subsequent administration accounts of events. Journalists might not be faulted though, if it were just information disclosed later that undermined the accounts they presented. Information presented the day before and within that day's article suggest the reported account is of questionable reliability. The day before it was reported that Secretary of State Shultz had claimed that there was no evidence that the Soviet pilots signalled or warned the jetliner and that there apparently existed no ability to communicate between the two aircraft. The *Times* further reported that while there existed established procedures for interceptors to warn straying aircraft at night, "[t]here was no indication whether any such exchange occurred" (September 2:4).

When the issue was Soviet efforts to communicate, the suggestion was that there was no evidence of communication and no ability to do so. When, the next day, the issue was Korean attempts to comply with Soviet instructions, the procedures to signal or communicate existed and were attempted. But evidence of such effort was, even according to officials, less than overwhelming:

The officials said that the exact nature of the Korean plane's action was not clear because Soviet descriptions were "incomplete" and intercepts of the Soviet conversations were "fragmentary" and were listened to after the event, not during it. (September 3:6)

Further difficulties with the reported official account were suggested though not pursued when in the same article it was acknowledged

[a]lthough they have not yet received a transcript of communications between the Korean plane and air traffic controllers in Japan, American officials said the conversation reportedly contained no hint of trouble. The officials said they could not explain why the Korean crew did not notify authorities they were being tracked by Soviet planes.

The situation was not simply that the crew did not report their circumstances to authorities. It might be imagined—at least by the reader—that the crew was too preoccupied with the pursuing fighter jets to communicate with ground controllers. The situation was instead that the crew was in communication with controllers and in that communication said nothing about the pursuing Soviet planes. It is no wonder that officials were unable to explain such a scenario. Despite obvious difficulties with the accounts provided by officials, the article went on to conclude that it was "apparent that the crew realized that they were being intercepted, according to the American officials." There was apparently little inclination to question or further examine this official account.

While the claim that the crew of Flight 007 was aware of the pursuit and attempted to signal their willingness to comply with Soviet demands was not critically examined, neither was it pursued in later reports. In fact, in a story in the next day's edition of the *Times* (September 4:17) where it was suggested that the crew of the passenger jet was unaware of the Soviet interceptors, the previous day's report was not reintroduced for scrutinization. A tape transcript of the Soviet pilot's communication to ground commanders, supplied by the Japanese Broadcasting Corporation, was quoted in the *Times* as follows: " 'It is now within sight. We have approached within two kilometers. The plane is not yet aware of us. We will continue pursuit.' Afterward the pilot reportedly said, 'Missile fired' and 'shot down.' " While it is possible that either the original transcript or the *Times* provided an edited version of the communication, if we assume no important part of the conversation is missing, it appears that the crew of 007 was not aware that they were being stalked.

As accounts continued, the story, and the official claims became more confusing. While the original claim of U.S. officials was that the crew of the Korean airliner was aware that they were being pursued and had attempted to communicate their willingness to comply with Soviet instructions, later their position was that the crew was unaware of their situation and that the Soviets never made an attempt to warn the intruding plane of the danger to which it was exposing itself. After a release of an earlier tape transcript seemed to conflict with the Soviet claim that their pilot had fired warning tracers across the path of the Korean plane when other attempts to get the attention of the plane failed, the State Department later released a revised transcript that provided "possible but inconclusive substantiation for Soviet contention" that warning shots had been fired (*NYT*, September 12:1). Of the three sections of the original transcript that were revised after "an extensive review of the tapes by linguistic experts," one was changed to quote the Soviet pilot as saying that he fired "cannon bursts" six minutes before launching the missiles that destroyed the plane. The article quoted State Department officials claiming that the shot may have been aimed at the plane rather than being meant as a warning.

A few months later in an article about how the United States was seeking censure of the Soviet Union by international aviation authorities, it was reported that there were no indications that warning shots had been fired "despite Soviet assertions" to the contrary (*NYT*, December 13:7). The *Times* again had ignored its own earlier reporting and adopted the official government position. The cannon fire, not noted in the later report, must have been intended to down and not warn Flight 007. It appeared then, according to the *Times*, that the Soviets made no effort to warn the intruding plane. While some articles appear to indicate some ambiguity regarding this matter, it was apparently concluded that the Soviets shot the plane down without making a prior effort to contact it.

Did Soviets Identify 007?

Since they had not communicated with the plane, it could not be immediately determined whether the Soviets had been able to positively identify the intruding plane. Again, the issue of identification is important if we are to understand the meaning of the Soviet attack. Examination of presentation of this issue can help to understand much about news presentation by the *Times*. In fact, presentation of this aspect of the story provides a striking example of how reports in the *Times* frequently include information that is inconsistent with the themes of its stories or the frames within which stories are reported and the official versions of events.

Usually buried within longer stories, but occasionally even headlined in brief articles, was an acknowledgment that intelligence officials were at least uncertain that the Soviets had known they were shooting down a civilian airliner and that instead they had misidentified the plane as a military flight that was intruding into their most sensitive defense areas. Full acknowledgment of this mistake might have required a redefinition of the event within the press. The matter might have to be seen as being more complicated than a simple act of murder by the representatives of a society that places little or no value on innocent human life. It would have been unlikely that a redefinition would have absolved the

Soviets of all blame in the matter. But it might have suggested a reinterpretation of the murderous intent attributed the act and a reinterpretation too of the necessary implications of a brutal, uncivilized society that would willfully commit such an act.

It therefore becomes interesting that the *Times* contained acknowledgment, though muted, early in its coverage of the incident, that officials unofficially acknowledged uncertainty as to whether the Soviet pilots had been able to identify the plane. It was reported that while intelligence officials believed that the pilots must have been able to identify their target as a passenger liner if they were able to make good visual contact with it, they were unable to determine from the transcripts if the pilots had been able to do so (September 4:18). While readers were informed in a story headlined "A Soviet General Implies Airliner May Have Been Taken for Spy Jet" (September 5:1), on the next day, after it was acknowledged that there had been an U.S. spy plane in the area of Flight 007's flight path, the readers were told under the headline "Congressional Leaders Discount Significance of the U.S. Spy Plane" that "Congressional leaders of both parties, after White House briefings and conversations with Reagan administration officials, played down the possibility that the Soviets could have confused the two aircraft" (September 6:15).

A day later the headline reported, "U.S. Says Soviet Contrives 'to Lie to the World' on Jet" (September 7:14). White House spokesperson Larry Speakes was quoted in this article as claiming that the administration had "further evidence" that provided " 'irrefutable' proof that the Russians knowingly shot down a civilian aircraft." Speakes, it was reported, refused to specify or describe the nature of the evidence in the interest of protecting intelligence sources. In the third to last paragraph of the story it was observed,

Under questioning, however, administration officials acknowledged that no absolute proof of Soviet intentions had yet been disclosed by the United States. The administration continues to maintain . . . "it strains credulity that the Russians could not know what they were doing."

Even at the end of the article then, after it was acknowledged that the administration was making claims that not only could it not support but were simply untrue, it was the administration's evaluation of credulity that is left to define the situation.

Later articles continued to provide suggestions that the Soviets did not realize they were shooting at a civilian plane. Western military attaches were identified as sources according to whom Flight 007 had not been positively identified (September 18:16), and a senior administration official was quoted as saying that it was "quite possible" that the Soviet fighter pilot had not known he was shooting at a civilian plane (September 18:17). Toward the end of September a short, four-paragraph article headlined "Soviet Delegate Admits Error in Plane Incident" reported that a low-level Soviet official, while attending a conference in England, said that Flight 007 had been mistakenly identified as a military reconnaissance plane. While he claimed that the civilian airliner was engaged in a spy mission, he said that the plane would not have been shot down if it was recognized to be a commercial airliner (September 22:3).

The relative position and sense of importance attributed to these reports was indicated by later treatment of the same issue in early October. A front-page headline declared, "U.S. Experts Say Soviet Didn't See Jet Was Civilian" (October 7:1). The implication was that some new discovery had been made with regard to the incident. In fact, a close reading of the *Times* since the shooting would have suggested the conclusions that suddenly merited front-page presentation. The single difference between the information reported on October 7, and the information reported earlier is the source, or more accurately, the manner in which the source spoke. The headline in October was reporting the official pronouncement of the government. Earlier articles, even though they provided the assessments of officials, reported unofficial and unattributed assessments. It was not the information or the source that was new in October, it was the government's manner of pronouncement that was new. This difference, in turn, influenced the *Times* presentation.

The article noted that information regarding the Soviets' failure to correctly identify Flight 007 had been presented to the White House and the State Department about two weeks after the incident. Days before this report appeared, however, President Reagan had called the attack a "crime against humanity" and claimed, "There is no way a pilot could mistake this for anything other than a civilian airliner." The administration, it was observed, had been calling the incident a breach of human rights. The implications were, first, that the administration, and particularly the President, had knowingly misrepresented the incident (at least to the degree they claimed Soviet recognition of their target) and, second, that the "new" evidence might necessitate a redefinition, or what we might call a reframing, of the incident. A State Department spokesperson apparently tried to maintain the original frame as he was quoted as claiming that shooting down an unarmed reconnaissance plane would be just as abhorrent as shooting down a commercial flight. Additionally, according to administration officials, even if the Soviets did not know the identity of the plane, they should have—"it was their business to know."

What began as an article providing or restating information that might limit Soviet blame in the incident was becoming an opportunity for government officials to restate their case against the Soviet Union. The article continued, that since the administration's initial response to the shooting "many new, important details have been gathered and analyzed, but the State Department and the White House have been reluctant to speak publicly about this." It was then observed, "The administration's reticence, officials said, is in part a result of an effort not to compromise American intelligence gathering activities and of a desire not to overshadow an investigation being undertaken by the International Civil Aviation Organization, a United Nations agency." It was not identified by either the *Times* or the administration how the continued release to the public of information known to be false—particularly in the face of public accessibility of more accurate information—protected U.S. intelligence operations.

In the treatment of the issues of both the Soviet warning of Flight 007 and Soviet identification of the plane, the *Times* seems quite consistent. In each case it frames the presentation of the issues in a manner quite similar to the government's official account while also including, though not highlighting, conflicting information. When conflicting information that initially appears to undermine the existing frames does receive attention, even when it is accompanied by direct criticism or critique of government pronouncements, the threat to official accounts is quickly defused in favor of further, even if facile, administration-supplied or oriented explanations.

Reliance on the source that has just been criticized to provide the definitive explanation or definition of the situation is an interesting phenomenon. But it does not necessarily indicate manipulative control or domination of the media by the government. It instead may simply be an indication of the strength of the sense of legitimacy with which the government is viewed in our culture. This sense of legitimacy will be exaggerated even more when the alternative understanding offered is seen to be consistent with Soviet purposes. We may recognize and laud domestic debate—at least as it remains within respectable and productive bounds—but Soviet reality, or a perspective understood to be consistent with Soviet interest, does not represent an alternative that challenges the official U.S. presentation of international issues. The most certain way to promote an official government explanation might be for the Soviets to counterpose it or for alternatives to be identified as being in the Soviet interest.

The *Times'* Paranoid Perpetuation of Conspiracy Theory

The one voice within the *Times* that consistently questioned the administration's explanation of the incident was that of Tom Wicker. Interestingly, he not only questioned the administration's story but also the treatment of that story by his journalist colleagues. Three and a half months after the incident, Wicker observed in his "In the Nation" column, that since the fall "new information has emanated from Washington itself to suggest that the Soviet action may not have been so wantonly brutal as was then depicted" (December 19:19). Rather than an intentional effort to destroy a civilian airliner, suggested Wicker, the incident can be best understood by recognizing that the Soviet forces thought they were shooting at a spy plane. That the Soviets misidentified the plane had been supported, according to the column, by both U.S. intelligence and the ICAO. Among the reasons for the Soviets to suspect a spy plane Wicker lists: a Soviet missile test had been scheduled for that night (this was one of the few acknowledgments of the planned test in the press), the practice of the National Security Agency of sometimes intentionally penetrating Soviet airspace, and the presence of an RC–135 in the area at the time. Wicker finally pointed out, "Even the ICAO report was unable to cite any but speculative reasons of crew error as to why Flight 007 was off course and over Soviet airspace for more than two hours."

A year after the incident the headline of Wicker's column was "A Damning Silence" (September 7, 1984:27). He observed then:

The depressing complicity with government into which the free American press has sunk since Vietnam and Watergate has seldom been more visible than it was at the first anniversary of the Soviet destruction of Korean Airlines Flight 007, on Sept. 1, 1983.

While the press and airwaves gave full report to Reagan administration statements,

[the] press effectively ignored an authoritative article in *The Nation* (for Aug. 18–25) establishing to a reasonable certainty that numerous agencies of the U.S. Government knew or should have known, almost from the moment Flight 007 left Anchorage, Alaska, that the plane was off course and headed for intrusion into Soviet air space, above some of the most sensitive Soviet military installations.

Evidence in *The Nation* article suggested "at least to the level of a high probability" that the plane had been permitted by U.S. intelligence to enter Soviet airspace in the interest of the "bonanza" of intelligence information that it would provide. U.S. responsibility does not require that the overflight was orchestrated. Rather,

the deliberate silence—or the shocking failure—of so many U.S. detection systems argue that President Reagan and the security establishment have greater responsibility for the fate of Flight 007 than they admit—or that a complaisant press has been willing to seek.

Wicker's column provoked a letter by Henry E. Catto, Jr., in response (October 2, 1984:30). Catto, a contributing editor to the *Washington Journalism Review* and a former Assistant Secretary of Defense, objected to Wicker's "swipe at journalistic colleagues" and claimed that accounts of *The Nation*'s article

appeared in major papers, on the wire services and on nightly TV, even before the article itself appeared, and Pearson [the author of the article] himself was on the "Today" show. If there has been a lack of interest, it is surely not due to a "complaisant press" but to the happy fact that most reporters and commentators quite properly dismissed Pearson's arguments for what they are: drivel.

Catto's letter further observed:

We have here a classic example of two facets of the American psyche: love of the idea of conspiracy, no matter how flimsy the evidence, and the peculiar readiness of many to assume the worst of our people and our Government.

Wicker's next consideration of the issue (October 21, 1984:D23) noted that no official or agency of the administration had yet offered a reply to the *Nation* article. He acknowledged Catto's letter but noted that rather than denying the charges and implications of the column, Catto "offered only renunciation and two general points, neither of which can stand the light of day." While Catto claimed that the ICAO had concluded pilot error was the cause of the Korean plane's flight path, Wicker pointed out that the ICAO had offered "only speculative reasons for this judgment" and that the Air Navigation Commission, in review of the ICAO report maintained that it could not validate any pilot error scenarios. Why, since U.S. military stations, according to the ICAO, knew that Flight 007 had been off course almost immediately from its departure from Anchorage, had not civilian air traffic controllers been notified? Such communication between the military and civilian controllers is required under the conditions of a 1972 agreement between the Pentagon and the Federal Aviation Commission.

The *Nation* article received the attention of the *Times* almost two months after the article originally appeared but three days after a full-page advertisement about the article appeared in the newspaper (October 28, 1984:3). Under the headline "Article on Downing of Jet is Disputed," Phillip Taubman reported that the *Nation* had claimed that Flight 007 had probably been tracked by the U.S. military, but had not been informed of its dangerous path and that no major U.S. press organization had investigated the administration's claims regarding the incident. In response to these claims, Taubman quoted the Assistant Secretary of State for European Affairs, Richard B. Burt, as asserting,

The *Nation* article is pure baloney. As far as I know—and I know a great deal about this case—I am aware of absolutely no evidence to suggest that any U.S. agency was aware that the Korean airliner was off course and over Soviet territory prior to being shot down.

Taubman added:

A variety of aviation and intelligence experts outside the government said that the plane's flight path might have registered on some of the military and intelligence radar systems, but that there was no established procedure at the time for quickly transmitting information to civilian aviation authorities.

In response to the claim that the reconnaissance plane that had been in the area was either part of a coordinated intelligence mission or at least knew of the presence of the Korean airliner in Soviet territory, Taubman quoted Admiral Bobby R. Inman, the former Deputy Director of the CIA and head of the National Security Agency, as saying that RC–135s were primarily equipped to monitor the reentry phase of Soviet missile tests and that they had the capability to track aircraft for defensive purposes. They would have been unable to monitor the Korean plane as it entered Soviet territory.

In response to the criticism of the press's coverage of the incident, Taubman quoted the managing editor of the *Washington Post*, Leonard Downie Jr., who explained,

the *Post*, like other major newspapers and TV networks investigated the flight of KAL 007 within an inch of its life. We were very open-minded and skeptical about what happened. We tracked down an amazing number of tips, including the kind mentioned in the *Nation* article, and they just didn't check out.

The *Times* apparently also participated in an exhaustive effort to research the incident. Taubman reported that following the shooting, the *Times* assigned six reporters to investigate the event, giving particular attention to the issues of the possible intention to spy and whether U.S officials could have warned the 007 crew. On the anniversary of the incident, two reporters were assigned to review the case. Taubman concluded his article by observing, "The reporters found no evidence to support assertions that United States authorities were in a position to warn the South Korean plane as it entered Soviet airspace."

For both claims reported to be central to the *Nation* piece, that U.S. officials could have or should have been able to warn the Korean airliner and that the news media did not investigate the incident, there seems, at least according to the treatment in the *Times*, to be little support. In fact, in the 15-paragraph article, after the initial two paragraphs that identified the *Nation*'s claims, the following 13 paragraphs were used to discredit those claims or present contradictory evidence. Considering the limited attention given the *Nation* article, this balance (or imbalance) of the piece in the *Times* that does deal specifically with the article is particularly interesting.

Taubman's piece apparently did not convince Wicker that all the significant questions about the incident had been investigated and answered. The week of the second anniversary of the incident, the "In the Nation" column was titled "A Disintegrating Story" (September 3, 1985:21). It was the administration's story of events surrounding the shooting of 007 that was described as disintegrating.

On the second anniversary of the shooting down of Korean Airlines Flight 007 on Sept. 1, 1983, it seemed clearer than ever that the truth of this terrible event, in which 269 lives were lost, has not yet been told. Facts keep turning up that won't fit the generally accepted version or that raise serious and unanswered questions about it.

Despite the continual identification of facts that raise unanswered questions about the administration's version of the story, that version, Wicker observed, is so widely accepted "that questioners are accused of being paranoid perpetrators of a conspiracy theory or even servants of Soviet interests."

Regardless of the dominant wisdom, "The conventional theory is inherently implausible and may be disintegrating." Wicker noted a series of observations and developments that are necessarily problematic to the maintenance of the administration's scenario. First was the concern apparently voiced by an American radar operator who said, "We should warn him," presumably in reference to the Korean jet. While the voice was said to be heard on a tape of conversations among radar operators, the government was unwilling to identify the voice to permit further investigation. Further, tapes that record radar trackings were destroyed within 30 hours of the flight of 007 despite their obvious importance to any investigation. While the tapes are recycled under routine conditions, the situation in question was certainly not routine. (Both of these issues were identified in an article that appeared in the *Times* two days before the Wicker column was published [September 1, 1985:3]. The article, headlined "U.S. Saw Korean Jet Stray, Suit Says," reported the evidence introduced in a lawsuit filed against the U.S. government by relatives of victims of the shooting.) Wicker additionally cited Japanese Prime Minister Nakasone's release of data from Japan Defense Agency monitors that tracked Flight 007 that "detailed significant changes of altitude and speed by the Korean plane while radio transmissions, ostensibly from its pilots, described quite different maneuvers." Wicker observed that the data suggested evasive action by the crew over Sakhalin while deceiving controllers and contradicts both the administration and the ICAO reports that maintain the crew was unaware they had entered Soviet airspace. While the administration claimed that the plane had flown a continuous straight-line course, to have flown over Sakhalin, Flight 007 must have made two turns. The data released make it seem "indisputable" that the plane did, in fact, change its course as suggested by critics of the administration's statements.

In a follow-up to his column three days earlier, Wicker's next "In the Nation" column examined the significance of a statement by Charles Lichtenstein, the deputy United States representative to the United Nations (September 6, 1985:23). Two days after the shooting down of 007, addressing the Soviet delegate in answer to whether Americans had tracked the flight, Lichtenstein responded, "No, I would assure the representative of the Soviet Union: We followed you following the flight." According to Wicker,

It's hard to understand how U.S. monitors could have tracked Soviet monitors as the latter tracked Flight 007, while the American monitors had no knowledge that Flight 007 was off course and in trouble: but the administration has not explained Mr. Lichtenstein's statement. A U.S. official, for example, was quoted as follows in *The Washington Post* on Feb. 24, 1985: "We have never explained that because it gets into intelligence information."

Wicker wondered, if Lichtenstein's statement had been a security breach, how could President Reagan's declaration three days after Lichtenstein spoke that "the Soviets tracked this plane for two and a half hours" be explained? Further, "if the U.S. knew so much about what the Russians were doing, how could it have known nothing of what Flight 007—the object of the Russian activity—was doing?"

In addition to the monitoring of Soviet monitors, U.S. intelligence had a host of other resources in place with which it should have been aware of the Korean airliner's course. Wicker quoted a report in the *Bulletin of Concerned Asian Scientists* that appeared the previous spring.

In a position to monitor some phases of the flight were at least one P-3 Orion Navy reconnaissance plane, several RC-135s, the frigate USS Badger, the reconnaissance ship USS Observation Island with its radar, "Cobra Judy" and, of course, the land-based facilities in Alaska, on Shemya Island ("Cobra Dane" and "Cobra Talon") in Hokkaido (the phased-array radar at Wakkauai) and main-island Japan (the mighty NSA listening post at the US Air Base at Misawa, near the northern tip of Honshu; the largest American listening post in Asia).

Such a collection of tracking and intelligence technology led Wicker to conclude, "That Flight 007 was not warned can be explained only by insisting that despite this array of electronic sentinels, no American knew the airliner was in trouble at any time during its 5 hour, 26 minute journey from Anchorage to disaster over Sakhalin."

About the ICAO report which was referred to by Catto and others as supporting the official U.S. scenario, Wicker observed that the investigation relied on unchallenged U.S. information—information that has since been clearly shown to require reevaluation. Further, this was only the second disaster inquiry in the history of the ICAO. The organization used a staff of five full-time and four part-time workers in the course of a 60-day investigation. In comparison, the National Transportation Safety Board required more than 100 people and seven months to investigate a 1979 crash at O'Hare Airport. Finally, the ICAO's own Air Navigation Commission concluded after the release of the report that "the magnitude of the diversion" from the intended flight path "cannot be explained" by the crew error stated in the study.

On Credibility and National Character

Wicker's was clearly a minority voice at the *Times*, and in the press generally. In his columns he was raising issues and asking questions that were not only avoided but seemingly inconceivable to other journalists. Wicker questioned the official statements of the administration, but also—and this is where his work is truly unique—considered the implications of the administration's practice of giving misleading or even false statements. Wicker's kind of skepticism was more commonly reserved for Soviet rather than U.S. announcements. (Even in his skepticism, Wicker weighs evidence more than is typical when the object of journalistic skepticism is a Soviet official explanation.)

Days after the 007 was shot down a *Times* story was headlined "Lost: Korean Jet, 269 Lives and Credibility" (September 4:Dl). The credibility noted was that of the Soviet Union. In support of the headline the story quoted President Reagan, who had asserted that the Soviets lost their credibility "when they so flagrantly lied" as they were doing in this instance. The article explained how Moscow was standing "information on its head" in its statements and explanations made with regard to the 007 incident. In contrast to the Soviet Union, which would stand information on its head and flagrantly lie, the West could be expected to provide a full, forthright, and honest accounting of events. In a story about knowledge among the Soviet citizenry of the 007 incident, it was reported that a number of people "learned the full story behind the incident by listening to Russian-language broadcasts from West Germany and Great Britain and from the Voice of America" (October 2:14). The Soviets misuse, distort, and manipulate news, but the West gives the full story. These seem to be some of the assumptions that provided the context within which journalists work.

The Soviet manipulation of news is only one instance of the horrific nature of that society. "[I]t took a special kind of mentality and political system to institute rules of engagement that would empower the military to destroy a civilian aircraft" (*NYT*, September 4:Dl). That we know the rules of engagement and that the aircraft in this case was identified as civilian are both problematic assumptions, but since we know the Soviets have a "special kind" of political system and society we tend not to recognize the problematics contained in our criticisms. Evidence for our conclusion, the nature of Soviet society, is actually a consequence of our conclusion. We "know" about Soviet society and therefore expect acts such as the wanton destruction of Flight 007. Our definition of the act reinforces our "knowledge." We all know that the Soviet Union is a "rigid, morbidly suspicious society" and that even after this incident the Soviets "still barely grasped what the humanitarian essence of Western life is all about" (September 11:D2). Our understanding of our own Western life and our understanding of Soviet life reinforce each other as polar opposites. A result is the pattern of news reporting that we witness in the *Times* and most other publications. When the issues are international and can be understood as having bilateral, U.S.–Soviet significance, we rely on our cultural knowledge to provide our orientation and insight. Our cultural knowledge has provided us with justification for our unfailing criticism and suspicion of the reality presented by Soviet officials and a similarly unwavering acceptance of and reliance on that reality presented by U.S. officialdom.

FROM OUT OF THE MAINSTREAM: *THE NATION*

As an indication that particular cultural knowledge or the hegemony of dominant ideology is neither absolutely uniform, nor necessary, accounts of the 007 incident from the alternative U.S. press and from the Canadian press will be considered.

The articles in *The Nation* were referred to above in the discussion of the *New York Times*. The August 18/25, 1984 and August 17/24, 1985 issues of the periodical each contained extended articles examining the 007 incident. The editors noted at the beginning of the first article that David Pearson, the investigator and author of the article

does not pretend to answer the question of whether KAL 007 was a spy plane, but he does answer two key questions—What did we know and when did we know it? By implication he raises further profoundly disturbing questions about just how open our society is when it comes to matters of alleged national security. Indeed, when it comes to matters Soviet, can we ever trust our leaders to tell us the truth? (August 18/25, 1984:105)

Clearly, such issues, raised either implicitly or explicitly, are not of the sort raised, or even recognized in the press thus far considered. Wicker's observation that Pearson's work received little media attention can, in part, be explained by the recognition that the issues Pearson addresses are not issues within "mainstream" media. Pearson's work need not be considered because it did not deal with legitimate issues. Some work is discredited not because it presents a too extreme or unbalanced treatment of an issue or topic, but because the issue or topic itself is beyond the realm of consideration. To consider such things is to be unreasonable. Indeed, it was Wicker who observed that those who expressed doubt about the administration's version of the incident were seen as "paranoid perpetrators of a conspiracy theory or even servants of Soviet interests" (*NYT*, September 3, 1985:21). An evaluation of Pearson's work need not measure the merits of the work itself—the quality of the investigation, the logic of his analysis—it can instead be determined to be "drivel" simply on the basis of the nature of the questions implied or acknowledged by the study itself.

For the purposes of the present work, the significance of the articles in *The Nation* is not whether they suggest conclusions beyond any doubt about the nature of Flight 007 or about a possible subsequent administration cover-up. The significance is instead in the example the articles represent of how the issue of the flight might have been treated and the manner in which the treatment was accomplished. The editors of *The Nation* have observed:

It is appropriate that a scholar whose areas of concentration are complex organizations and communication, rather than a member of the traditional press (which was quick to accept the administration's version of what happened), should be the one to break this extraordinary story. (August 18/24, 1984:105)

They might have added that it was not only appropriate but, quite possibly, necessary that a journalist not be the one to accomplish the investigation and write the story. Journalists, having their stable of "reliable" sources would have depended on those "highly placed" sources for information and verification. Indeed, sources from within the intelligence establishment were repeatedly cited as the definitive and authoritative voice in answer to any and all questions regarding the incident—even when those answers were acknowledged to be found wanting. It would be necessary to plumb other sources if questions were to be responded to in anything but the official manner.

Rather than relying on official government spokespeople, Pearson, who was writing his dissertation on the Department of Defense's World Wide Military Command and Control System, made extensive use of technical literature. Using that literature and a variety of other sources, Pearson concluded,

> Various U.S. military and intelligence agencies . . . had to have known that Flight 007 was off course well prior to the attack over Sakhalin. . . . Those agencies had to have known that KAL 007 was heading toward Soviet territory while a major Soviet missile test was in the making there. . . . The agencies had the time and means to communicate with KAL 007. . . . It seems probable that Soviet radar systems were jammed . . . given the capability of U.S. intelligence and communications systems, it can be presumed that the White House and the Secretary of Defense also knew of the events as they transpired. (August 18/25, 1984:105)

The technical literature with which Pearson began his research was available to the journalists of the traditional press. While Pearson was probably more familiar with the literature than most people because of his dissertation research, any journalists who were interested in attempting to substantiate or verify their reports had the opportunity to wade through the same material.

Work of the kind that Pearson accomplished is the product of investigative research that might be difficult to manage for a reporter assigned to keep up with a fast-breaking story. It is clear, though, that Pearson, from the start, did not share the assumptions that seem to have characterized most reporting of the incident. These assumptions, rather than the lack of time or resources, seem to explain the different approaches to the story. Indeed, it is claimed that the press had investigated the flight of 007 to "within an inch of its life." (See, for example, the quote of Leonard Downie, Jr., the managing editor of the *Washington Post*, cited above.)

CANADIAN VIEWS

Further indication of how journalistic, or more accurately cultural, assumptions shaped the presentation of events surrounding the flight of KAL 007 can be illustrated by looking at how the incident was presented in the press outside of the United States. While we might expect the incident to be almost unrecognizable in its presentation in the press of East bloc nations, we would expect the objective accounts in the free press of Western democracies to be quite similar to each other. It could be informative then to compare accounts in the U.S. press with those found in the press of another Western nation. The geographical and cultural proximity of the United States and Canada might lead us to expect minimal differences in the presentation of Flight 007 by the press of the two nations. That citizens of both countries were aboard the flight would further suggest the likelihood of similarities in press treatment. Examples of the Canadian press examined here include the weekly magazine *Maclean's* and the *Globe and Mail*, self-described as "Canada's National Newspaper."

Maclean's

The first issue of *Maclean's* after the shooting of Flight 007 presented the incident as its cover story (September 12, 1983). The magazine's cover had a painting of a Soviet plane firing a missile at a KAL plane that was yet to be destroyed. The cover was titled "Flight Into Darkness." The cover and much of the presentation on the pages inside the magazine communicated a reaction of horror and anger in response to the incident. A "worldwide wave of revulsion and rage" was reported and it was noted "In the aftermath, the most compelling single question was why an unarmed, off-course civilian airliner was so ruthlessly destroyed" (September 12:18). But in contrast to the American newsweeklies *Maclean's*, both in tone and in content, presented the incident more ambiguously.

In the third paragraph of the cover story the question of how the Korean plane could have strayed so far off course was raised by *Maclean's* writers. Failure of all three navigational computer systems was described as "a one-in-a-million possibility," and the procedure for the independent programming of each computer was described. It was also noted that warnings of the dangers of navigational errors appeared on maps used by the crew and that CP Air had flown the same route six times weekly for the past 34 years without incident (September 12:19). The next page included a photo of a "Korean Airlines Boeing 747: equipped with fail safe navigational equipment."

While Secretary of State Shultz's account of events was presented, it was also noted that it was clearly

possible that the Korean plane strayed into Soviet airspace as part of a continuing game of cat and mouse played by the superpowers around the world. The purpose of the exercise is not to take photographs but to provoke a response. The radio traffic and radar emissions from the other side's activities are closely monitored to measure reaction time and the numbers and types of planes that take to the air to intercept. (September 12:20)

Here *Maclean's* has made two acknowledgments that were never noted in the American magazines. First, it is suggested that civilian planes are used by both the Soviet Union and the United States to provoke a reaction by the other side. While it was noted in *Time* and *Newsweek* that Soviet planes frequently wandered, it was denied that U.S. authorities would ever consider endangering innocent lives in this manner. Further, the American magazines, in an effort to indicate the absurdity of using passenger planes in an effort to gather intelligence, repeatedly reported that such flights would be worthless, given the sophisticated photographic and reconnaissance technology that U.S. intelligence forces had at its disposal. (It was not explained why the Soviets, in contrast to the Americans, required such flights.) Additionally, it was reported, it would have been impossible to equip a 747 with the hardware that would be required to make the plane of any use in gathering intelligence. The possibility that the plane could play any role in an effort coordinated with other reconnaissance resources—the scenario suggested as a clear possibility in *Maclean's*—was not considered or even mentioned in the American weeklies. (It was noted in the *New York Times* [September 11, 1983:18] that this issue had been raised by "nonmilitary experts on electronic warfare," but it was discounted as "not probable," as the locations of radar installations had been registered by past RC–135 flights and photographed by satellites.) The scenario suggested in *Maclean's* was given additional credence by a report in the British magazine *Defence Weekly* (cited in *The Nation*, August 17/24, 1985), where it was suggested that among the monitoring resources available to U.S. intelligence in a coordinated effort to gather information was a Ferret-D satellite that was in position as Flight 007 made both its penetrations into Soviet territory to intercept electronic emissions from Soviet defense forces (August 18/25, 1984:117). While the specific information about the satellite might not have been immediately available to journalists, the history upon which *Maclean's* based its suggestion of 007's involvement in an ongoing game of cat and mouse was available even to those journalists who wrote for *Time* and *Newsweek*. That this explanation for 007's flight path was not considered, and that instead any intelligence connection was emphatically denied, seems based more on our understanding of ourselves as Americans than on available evidence.

After considering the possibility of intentional provocation of Soviet defense forces, it was suggested in the *Maclean's* article that the military forces in the Soviet Far East are some of the "principal U.S. targets" and that the trespassed Sea of Okhotsk "holds particular interest," as it is the location of Soviet missile sites and tests (September 12:20). The area, it was noted, had been cited in a recent U.S. Defense Department report as a region of intensified activity to further build up Soviet military capabilities (September 12:21).

Maclean's also questioned the manner in which the U.S. administration responded to the flight of the Korean airliner. It reported that "One of the most puzzling aspects of the disaster was the fact that the plane's destruction was kept secret from the world for about 17 hours" (September 12:21). The political implications of this delay of public acknowledgment were not clear, but the misleading and erroneous reports of the well-being of the flight's passengers did obviously have an unfortunate effect on relatives.

The issue of whether U.S. intelligence followed the path of Flight 007 was also attended to in the first issue of *Maclean's* after the shooting. Again, *Maclean's* raised issues ignored by the U.S. magazines and treated issues acknowledged by both nations' magazines more critically. It was noted that in addition to listening posts in Japan that would have made it possible for U.S. intelligence forces to intercept the first Soviet responses to the intruder, there was a recently negotiated National Security Administration post in China that provided additional reconnaissance capabilities. With the array of intelligence resources available to the Americans, "an intelligence source in Washington" told *Maclean's*, "You can assume that a decoded English translation of the Soviet pilot's conversation with his ground control was on the duty officer's desk at NSA within 10 minutes of the pilot speaking." The article continued,

It is also likely that from the initial stages of the crisis, NSA satellites were directed to photograph the area constantly, and photographs may exist of the missile striking the airliner. What is not clear is whether the Americans tried to warn the KAL aircraft that it was off course, and, if not, why. (September 12:21)

Clearly, in its first reports of the 007 incident, the Canadian magazine indicated an attitude toward the events reported that was, in significant ways, dissimilar from its American counterparts. While the statements and explanations of U.S. officials were reported, those statements were not understood to provide the definitive account of events. The *Maclean's* account, at least initially, indicated an understanding of the world, and international relations in particular, that was more than a simple division into dichotomous forces. Rather than presenting the flight of the Korean airliner as a simple tale of good versus evil, or innocence versus moral bankruptcy, significant aspects of the flight were presented as being uncertain, and the meaning of events was suggested to be clouded by doubt and ambiguity. This presentation was quite different from that found in *Time* and *Newsweek*. At the very least, this is an indication that the press in Western democracies need not necessarily maintain the assumptions of legitimacy without accountability that are evident in the treatment of administration spokespeople in the American press when the issue presented is understood to have superpower significance.

The following week's issue of *Maclean's* seemed to lack much of the critical analysis that had characterized the previous issue. Most of the coverage of the 007 incident in the September 19 issue was given to the presentation of Washington's statements of the incident. While Soviet claims—such as the "sacred" nature of their airspace, their inability to identify 007 as a civilian aircraft, and involvement of the U.S. RC–135—were noted, they were always followed by a response or counterclaim provided by the U.S. administration (September 19:32). Soviet explanations for the events were characterized as "the Kremlin's belligerent rationale" (September 19:33) while the Reagan administration was seen to be acting in a statesmanlike manner.

Without gloating, the White House noted that the Soviet action had shocked, but not surprised, the administration. Public anger, meanwhile, was almost palpable. (September 19:33)

President Ronald Reagan won high marks for his administration's restrained handling of the incident. The only criticism came from the Republican right, which lamented the mildness of the retaliatory measures. (September 19:33)

Even with the presentation of U.S. explanations and favorable assessments of Reagan administration policy as the dominant theme of representation, *Mac-*

lean's provided a more textured or varied picture than that provided in the U.S. weeklies. The Canadian magazine attended more to inconsistencies and contradictions in the reports from U.S. and Japanese authorities (for example, a discussion of the confusion over the content and existence of tapes of communication between Soviet pilots and their ground controllers [September 19:34]) than the American magazines and, more significantly, acknowledged issues barely mentioned or ignored in *Time* and *Newsweek*.

Of all the issues surrounding the shooting down of KAL 007, *Maclean's* suggested the "most intriguing of all were claims and denials that the Korean airliner was on an intelligence-gathering mission" (September 19:34). The magazine reported, in contradiction to the analysis presented in the American news magazines, that "Experts dismissed the theory that KAL's Flight 007 strayed off course accidentally" (September 19:34). If not an accident, the plane's flight path must have been purposeful. The only scenario considered in *Time* or *Newsweek* involving purposeful flight into Soviet airspace suggested that the crew of the plane had attempted a short cut in an effort to save fuel. *Maclean's* seemed to imply something more sinister. "[T]here was no doubt that the KAL jet entered a highly sensitive Soviet military zone at an apparently critical time" (September 19:34). The timing was critical because the Soviets had scheduled a major missile test at the time of the overflight. *Time* and *Newsweek* apparently did not see the missile test as being of any potential importance, as they did not acknowledge it. The implications suggested in the *Maclean's* report were tempered somewhat by reference to 007's flight path as an "impenetrable technical riddle" (September 19:34). The magazine still, however, presented a less stridently anti-Soviet scenario than was found in the American magazines. While the American accounts were rather one-dimensional in their jingoistic reporting, *Maclean's* reported in a bit more detached and less virulent manner that allowed the consideration or at least the acknowledgment of evidence and ambiguities that permitted the story to be less conclusive.

The *Globe and Mail*

Like *Maclean's*, which provided a presentation of events less certain and more ambiguous than its American counterparts, the *Globe and Mail*, while somewhat inconsistent in its presentation, was less conclusive in its reporting than the *Times* had been. Much of the reporting in the *Globe and Mail* was essentially the presentation of the position of the Washington administration. But other perspectives were noted on a routine basis, and occasionally the presentation of extraordinary accounts articulating issues or perspectives that never found their way onto the pages of the American press were considered here.

The first account of the Korean airline incident to appear in the *Globe and Mail* reported that the plane had landed on Soviet Sakhalin Island (September 1:1). The safe landing had been reported by a South Korean Foreign Ministry spokesperson, who claimed the information had been supplied by U.S. intelligence. The report had been confirmed by the brother of Congressman Lawrence McDonald, who was quoted as having said the State Department had told his family that the plane had landed and was safe.

By next day's issue, the *Globe and Mail* was reporting the shooting down of the plane and its repercussions. On the front page were two articles about the incident. The headline and subhead of one story, "U.S. to study sanctions over jet" and "Soviet statement on shooting rejected," indicated the nature of the coverage. The article was primarily a presentation of statements by a spokesperson for the U.S. State Department. The first five paragraphs reported the American statements and information about the Canadians involved. The next three paragraphs provided information about the statement issued by the Soviets. The other front-page article reported the response of Canadian External Relations Minister Jean-Luc Pepin to developments. The theme of Pepin's position was that "We must keep things in perspective. But we must also show the Soviet Union that we are taking a firm stand and that we would like an explanation" (September 2:21). The article raised a series of issues that suggested—in a manner consistent with the next day's editorial—that the response of the Canadian government was, at least initially, being "cautious to a fault" (September 3:6). The structure of the article was such that questions were raised in regard to Pepin's statements, but then his responses to the issues raised were provided. Pepin was usually provided then, in effect, the last word. Other headlines from the day's issue of the newspaper (September 2:12) illustrate the range of directions and perspectives from which the incident was presented in the *Globe and Mail*: "Japanese kept back news of attack on Korean jet"; "Law not clear on such attacks, professor says"; "Airliner 'continued journey,' Tass says"; "Soviets 'paranoid' about trespassing"; "U.S. has few retaliatory cards to play" (labelled analysis); " 'Very wide margin' between flight path, restricted territory"; and " 'No excuse for this appalling act,' Shultz says of Soviets' air attack."

The following day's front-page headlines about the incident were increasingly critical of the Soviet Union. One headline reported, "Soviets liars, terrorists, U.S. President charges," and the other said "Canada seeks compensation for victims of 'massacre' " (September 3:1). The first two paragraphs of the first article illustrate the tone reporting seemed to have taken in the *Globe and Mail*.

President Ronald Reagan denounced the Soviets yesterday as terrorists and liars before meeting security advisers to plot further responses to the downing of a South Korea jetliner that flew into Soviet airspace.

Mr. Reagan stepped up his war of words only minutes before Moscow acknowledged—about 48 hours after the jetliner disappeared—that its jet fighters had "fired warning shots with tracer shells along the flying route" of what they believed to be a spy plane, and expressed "regret in connection with the human victims" of what it called an accident.

The article also reported that a State Department official had called it "totally inconceivable that the KAL plane had been involved in an intelligence mission and that there has been a history of Soviet flights into restricted American airspace to which the U.S. had responded with a warning or suspension of Soviet landing rights in the U.S." (September 3:2). In this context most anything the President and his security advisers plot in response to the Soviet action might seem reasonable and justified.

Reporting in the *Globe and Mail* continued, for a couple of days, in the same vein. There were also, though, obvious and startling departures from form. On the same page as an article, headlined "Attack called sign of barbaric Soviet ways," reporting a speech by Assistant Secretary of the U.S. Air Force Tidal McCoy, there also appeared a passenger's account of his flight, three years earlier, to South Korea (September 5:4). The account, that of a journalist, recalled how, during his flight, the plane was darkened, passengers were told to pull their window shades closed, and the plane's navigational lights were turned off. It had been suggested that the measures were due to the flight's proximity to Soviet territory. The journalist reported that "I didn't put any faith in that—at the time."

By itself, the journalist's account might have little meaning or even suggest that the Soviets willfully shoot at anything flying even close to their territory. In the context of the exchange of claims, denials, and counterclaims between the Soviet Union and the United States, the account can be understood to challenge the American position. The administration claimed that KAL 007 had its navigational lights on and was therefore readily identifiable as a civilian airliner. If, instead, it is the practice of passenger jets to turn their navigational lights off and provide no hint of their identity, or even existence, the Soviet claim that the plane flew without lights and was impossible to identify must be given added credence. Further, a question might be raised about why passenger planes fly in such a manner. Why would civilian planes in international airspace want to be difficult to visually contact and identify? One suggestion, given the context of events within which the article was placed, might be that the journalist's flight was not through international airspace, but instead, like Flight 007, within Soviet territory. Without visual contact the Soviets might hesitate—but as the world found out, not refrain from—shooting down an unidentified plane. Such flights, believed to be in little or limited danger, could be used to provoke a defensive posture by the Soviets and thereby provide important intelligence information for the West. Such a scenario would be consistent with Soviet claims about Flight 007. The short article in the *Globe and Mail* then is quite provocative and out of character with what had been appearing in the newspaper during the previous few days.

An even more obviously provocative article, and one that supports the scenario developed from the earlier article, appeared in the *Globe and Mail* two days later. The article, headlined "Airline passengers regularly put at risk, defense editor says," began by reporting, "South Korea has regularly put passengers at risk by using airliners as flying spy stations, an expert on defense electronics said yesterday" (September 7:12). The expert was Ernest Volkman, the national security editor of *Defence Science Magazine*. Volkman was quoted as observing,

"The plane's mission was just too obvious to the Russians. What happened to Flight 007 was inevitable." Noting the areas that the plane trespassed, Volkman reported that it was difficult to believe it had simply gotten lost. He also explained the special and unique capabilities of a passenger jet used to gather intelligence.

A "black box" recorder in the cargo hold of a jetliner can record frequencies of radio and radar signals in areas it is passing over. This digital recording is fed into a computer that sorts through the readings and picks out information of military value. Frequencies are changed regularly and the information must be updated every few weeks.

According to Volkman, "An amazing amount of information can be picked up from one of these flights. From an intelligence point of view this is top priority, for instance for jamming radios." Other methods of gathering intelligence, such as the use of high-flying spy planes or satellites, cannot get the same quality of information.

Information of the sort provided by Volkman was never presented in *Time*, *Newsweek*, or the *New York Times*. In fact, it was repeatedly denied that 007 could serve any intelligence function at all. In the *Globe and Mail* it was not only acknowledged that the flight could play an irreplaceable role in gathering intelligence, but also that such flights are flown on a routine basis. Even if Volkman's testimony is contestable it needs to be, in a press freely examining and presenting the world, contested rather than ignored. It is doubtful that Volkman is the only source for such information. In a press free from the constraints of an aggressive government and the de facto constraints of an oppressive ideological myopia, such information would find its way onto the pages of that press. We know the American press is legally free, but it does not seem free of the constraints imposed by the domination of the political culture by a hegemonic ideology that requires the world polarized into opposing camps of good and evil.

The article in the *Globe and Mail* presenting Volkman's analysis did not mark a point of significant change in the nature of the newspaper's reporting of the 007 incident. The information was not integrated into subsequent articles or used to cast doubt on alternative explanations of events. (One reason for this is the degree of reliance of the *Globe and Mail* on the wire services. The article about Volkman was written by a staff reporter, Wallace Immen, and did not come off the wire.) During the next week, until the middle of September, there was a mix of stories not unlike those that appeared in the first week after the shooting. One particular article appearing during the second week is interesting to note, however, particularly in the context of the article by Immen some days earlier. The article was labeled as analysis and headlined "Specialists ridicule spy charge" (September 12:1). The article is interesting in a number of respects. It came from the New York Times Service. It had appeared the previous day in the *Times* and was written by Drew Middleton, the *Times* military affairs correspondent. The article made reference to the capabilities of U.S. reconnaissance planes and satellites—they can photograph the bolts on the deck of a Soviet carrier or the newspaper being read by a man—suggesting that there would be no need to engage a civilian airliner in a spy mission that could accomplish nothing that other intelligence resources could do better. In the *Times* the Middleton piece appeared on page 18. In the *Globe and Mail* the piece was presented on the front page. It does not seem that it was used in the Canadian newspaper as a rebuff to the Immen article, which had appeared on page 12 five days earlier. It seems likely that the timing of the articles was coincidental; the relative placement of the articles seems unlikely to have been. *New York Times* material rates the front page in the *Globe and Mail*; *Defence Science Magazine* does not rate such status.

Such differences in the status or legitimacy of sources has the unavoidable effect of promoting one view of the world over others. When the stature of the *Times* is respected, so are the biases of the political culture it represents. Middleton did not deal with the issues raised by Volkman (nor would we have expected him to), yet his was seen as the authoritative voice that rated front-page presentation. The issues to which he did respond and those which he raised were identified as the important and legitimate or serious ones. While the Canadian press examined here is significantly different from the American press, it is not independent. The issues of the debate were still dominated though not controlled by the official U.S. definition of the situation. This definition was maintained, in part, by reliance on news services such as that provided by the *Times*. Such reliance is the result of the relative resources of each news organization, but also of the authority with which the *Times* is viewed. This respect for and influence of the *Times* have then, of course, become mutually reinforcing.

Despite such influences, the Canadian press examined here is clearly different from the American press. While pieces such as that by Immen are exceptional in the Canadian press, they are nonexistent in the United States. We can imagine journalists, even if they might consider doing such a piece (an unlikely possibility), deciding not to risk their position by submitting such a suggestion to an editor. The journalist, like the newspaper that would print it, would suffer serious damage to his/her credibility by writing such an article within the context of a political culture that encourages such work to be dismissed as "drivel" and the authors to be accused of loving conspiracy theories and assuming the worst of our people and government.

The Canadian press differentiates itself from its American counterparts even without its exceptional pieces. *Maclean's* and the *Globe and Mail* both framed their presentations of the 007 incident as an arena of superpower contest. While they, particularly the *Globe and Mail*, also absorbed the dominant American frame of good versus evil, they were also able to maintain, somewhat, the perspective of a spectator that could view the vulnerabilities that each of the opponents was attempting to conceal (from each other and/or themselves?) in their presentation of selves. It is this spectatorlike perspective—an interested detachment—that might be understood to be the stance or position that an "objective" press strives for. It is clear from the comparison of American press with

Canadian that while neither was able to claim detachment, the American press was more distant from the journalistic ideal. The implications of this failure are important to an understanding of the press, and of American society.

Next, a press will be examined that we can anticipate will be furthest from the American ideal of a detached, objective journalism. Below, the presentation of the shooting of Flight 007 in the Cuban weekly *Granma* will be examined. We would expect the official organ of the Central Committee of the Communist Party of Cuba to present a world quite different from the one found on the pages of the American and Canadian presses. The nature of the differences in presentation, along with any similarities that might be found, can provide an additional understanding of our own press and its place in our society.

THE CUBAN VIEW

On the second page of the September 11, 1983 issue of *Granma* appeared a full-page article titled "Disinformation and Mass Deception." The article, co-authored by William Preston, Jr., identified as the president of FOIA Inc. and the chair of the History Department of John Jay College of Criminal Justice in New York, and Ellen Ray, the editor of *Our Right to Know* and co-editor of *Covert Action Information Bulletin*, provided a historical perspective of "official U.S. deception operations against its own people." Progressing from "The Overt Era of Information Abuse, 1898–1945" to the subsequent era when "Information Goes Underground," the article cites repeated examples of the systematic use of disinformation and mass deception by the U.S. government.

On the next page of the same issue appeared an article headlined "White House and State Department Unleash Flagrant Anti-Soviet Campaign on Missing South Korean Airplane." The article, datelined Moscow, September 3, and released by *Tass*, was the first acknowledgment of the 007 incident. While it would be impossible to state with certainty the motivation or intention behind the relative placement of the two articles, it does seem that the reader is provided the message that the matter on page 3 is simply the most recent of the series of incidents, the systematic pattern, discussed on the previous page.

The *Tass* report observed that, in its statements about the incident, the U.S. administration resorted to "floods of gross slander." President Reagan's speeches, it was reported, were "filled with rabid, frenzied hatred for the USSR and socialism, cloaked in grand statements about 'humanism' and 'lofty sentiments.' " "The chief of the White House" was described as "shedding crocodile tears over what has happened." The report in *Granma* further explained that the motivation behind the incident, the purpose of the territorial intrusion, was obvious. "The aim of the provocation using the plane is very clear. But the Soviet Union and its people will not be discredited, which is what the Washington administration is trying to do now with particular fury. The irrefutable evidence will expose its plans. Slander cannot erase the traces of dishonorable acts."

Presentation of evidence of the dishonorable acts consists of two sorts: the unwillingness of the administration to respond to fundamental questions about the incident, and information gathered from Western news media. The questions left unanswered include:

Why did the plane enter Soviet airspace and depart from the established international route by a distance of up to 500 kilometers? Why did authorities of the United States and Japan, whose control services direct flights through this route and who knew that the plane was inside Soviet airspace for a long time, refrain from taking measures to end this brutal violation of the Soviet Union's sovereignty?

Interestingly, the *Tass* report claims that these questions had been raised by American journalists. Government spokespeople, though, had avoided answering the questions that must be answered if it is to be determined "Who sent the plane into Soviet airspace and for what purpose?"

A pattern that is apparent in the first report of the Korean airliner incident that would continue throughout the *Granma* material (and, since the reports in *Granma* originated almost exclusively in *Tass*, a pattern of reporting consistent in the *Tass* material examined) is an indication of the assumption that the evils of the United States are located in the character of its administration and not the American people—or its press. American journalists were asking the appropriate questions—it was the administration that was refusing to answer. It was the administration that had planned the provocative and brutal violation of Soviet territory, it was the administration that was expressing rabid, frenzied hatred for the Soviet Union and socialism, and it was the administration that was obstructing press efforts to identify the truth. The image of the American or, more generally, the Western press and its seemingly tireless effort to identify the truth is communicated, in part, by the reliance in *Tass* reports on the Western press for information. In the first article about the 007 incident alone there were repeated citations of "French TV," "the French TV network TF-1," "the *New York Times*," "the Japanese Kyodo Tsushin Agency," "Australian newspapers," "the Australian daily *Sydney Morning Herald*," "the Australian ABC radio and TV network," "BBC broadcasts," and "Western press reports." This pattern is repeated throughout the reports in the Cuban newspaper. The use of the work of Western journalists by *Tass*, and, subsequently, in *Granma* serves a dual purpose. First, it presents an image of Western governments, particularly that of the United States, as being irresponsive to the concerns of its press and people—even to the point of necessitating journalistic investigation that eventually threatens government claims. Second, reliance on such reports permits Havana, and by extension Moscow, from directly acknowledging what they knew about the incident. Eastern intelligence is protected by relying on Western press, thereby divulging little, if any, information of its own origin.

When not relying on the reports of Western journalism, reporting in *Granma* most often communicated the official statements and press conferences of government authorities. An example of this is the *Tass* release in *Granma* headlined "Provocative Policy" that appeared immediately below the first article on the KAL 007 shooting. The article quotes a statement by Colonel General Semian Romanov, the Head of the General Staff of the Soviet Antiaircraft Defence Troops. In Romanov's statement, the Korean airliner's penetration into Soviet airspace was characterized as "a premeditated and gross action." It was also observed that "in violation of the International Civil Aviation Organization's standards, navigation and collision prevention lights were not on. The crew of the intruding plane did not react to any of the actions of [the] intercepting plane whose pilot made repeated attempts over a long period of time to lead the plane to the nearest Soviet airport."

The following week's issue of *Granma* included the transcript of the press conference held by Marshal Nikolai Ogarkov, Chief of General Staff of the Soviet Armed Forces (September 18:3). The article, headlined "Soviet Detailed Report on Tendentious U.S. Maneuver with South Korean Plane," had a *Tass* byline. In light of the importance of the shooting, it was reported, the Soviet authorities had immediately "constituted a highly competent special state commission" that included "noted specialists and experts." Ogarkov detailed the flight of 007 in three stages from when it was first detected by Soviet radar (already 500 kilometers off course but still within the tracking zone of U.S. control services and antiaircraft defense systems) through its flight toward "the most important base of the strategic nuclear forces of the Soviet Union" (when the plane did not respond to Soviet communication but did emit coded signals of the sort used to transmit secret information) to its passage over Sakhalin Island, when "the transgressor plane's actions were challenging," where it changed direction and altitude, "abruptly" changing its course toward other military objectives. The crew of the intruding plane ignored repeated attempts to force it to land and the "preventative" bursts totaling 120 tracer bullets that were fired across the plane's path. Ogarkov concludes that it is "clearly evident" that the flight was "a reconnaisance operation thoroughly planned beforehand."

The next week an article written by *Tass* correspondent Igor Ignatiev was headlined, "Former CIA Director Says USSR Told Truth in Case of South Korean Spy Plane" (September 25:3). The subhead of the article explained, "Stansfield Turner says he could not swear on the Bible that the South Korean plane was not involved in espionage activity." This article, again, makes great use of material that appeared in the Western press. An Associated Press report that experts who had been commissioned by the Reagan administration to prove the claim that Soviet fighters had not attempted to establish contact with 007 had, in fact, proven the opposite was cited. This seems to be a reference to the analysis of the tapes of Soviet pilots and their ground controllers. The article reports that "according to AP, such prestigious evidence destroys the foundation upon which the U.S. administration's version rests." Additionally, the article cites a report by Newt Royce of the Hearst newspaper chain that quoted representatives of the U.S. intelligence service as saying that civilian airplanes are regularly used for espionage, and Denver *Post* reports that quote former U.S. intelligence officials as claiming that administration accounts are "full of holes and designed to fool public opinion."

In a four-paragraph article immediately below the one written by Ignatiev, it was observed that it had been reported in *Krasnaya Zvezda* (referred to as "The Organ of the Soviet armed forces") that the CIA had been using commercial planes on espionage missions over Soviet territory for the past ten years. The CIA and the South Korea airline, it was reported, had signed a "top secret agreement" during the early 1970s which provided use of specially equipped Boeing 747s that were to be used to gather intelligence over Soviet territory. The KAL pilots were specially trained for their task by Boeing and McDonnell Douglass. The head of KAL, Lee Hi Sung, it was noted, is "notoriously pro-U.S. and personally connected with U.S. secret services."

A third article, this one only two paragraphs long, appeared on the same page. This short piece continued the pattern of earlier reports. It was absolute in its criticism of the spy mission and used the Western press as its source of confirming information. After asking the question, "Why Didn't the RC–135 Warn the South Korean Plane?" in the headline, it was reported that the Japanese newspaper *Yumiuri* had claimed that the reconnaissance aircrafts are equipped to communicate with both military and civilian aircraft. There was also note, again, of the report in the Denver *Post* that quoted former intelligence officials saying that spy flights were routinely used to provoke Soviet responses that could be monitored.

Granma's final attention to the KAL incident was in the form of two articles the following week (October 2:3). The matter did not receive the attention of the Cuban newspaper for the rest of the year. The longer of the articles in the first week of October was headlined "South Korean Plane Delayed in Anchorage to Coincide with U.S. Spy Satellite." The article, from *Tass*, quoted Air Marshal Piotr Kirsanov as suggesting that while according to airline officials Flight 007's 40-minute delay at the Anchorage airport was to check onboard equipment, the delay was actually made necessary by a need to coordinate the flight's arrival over Kamchatka and Sakhalin with the path of the U.S. spy satellite Ferret-D. (This same suggestion was made, in greater detail, in the work of David Pearson presented in *The Nation*.) Additional evidence of the purpose of the flight included the restatement that there were more than the usual number of reconnaissance planes in the area, and 29 rather than the usual 18 crew members aboard the Boeing 747. Suspicions regarding the purpose of the flight were further fueled by reference to a study by British civil aviation officials that concluded, according to Kirsanov, that "it was absolutely impossible for such a plane to stray so far off course as a result of errors and defects in the plane's systems."

The second of the articles in *Granma* of October 2, headlined "Dispatch from Spanish News Agency," was a short piece again presenting claims of the two former intelligence officials that originally appeared in the Denver *Post*. There was no information in this article that had not appeared earlier in *Granma*, but the source cited here, seemingly important enough to be noted in the headline, was a Spanish news agency. Reference to information provided by the press outside of the East bloc sphere seems to be understood to provide greater credibility to the Soviet version of events.

There are at least two patterns in the reporting of *Granma* that are particularly notable. First, as mentioned above, there was repeated reference to reports of Western journalists in the Soviet news service and Cuban newspaper. As noted, there could be a strategic intelligence motivation for this. Soviet intelligence does not acknowledge their own capabilities or knowledge, but is still able to present evidence for its perspective by providing information in this manner. It would be necessary to examine the presentation of a number of issues or events to determine whether this is a common practice in Soviet or Cuban reporting.

The second pattern identified in *Granma* is related to the first, but has significance of a different sort. Both in its practice of using the reports of Western journalists and in the content and manner of its own reporting, *Granma* presented an image of the West—and particularly the United States—that draws sharp distinction between the administration or government, and the people. In the article of September 11, about the systematic use of disinformation and deception in the reporting of U.S. interference in Latin America, the impression is provided that the U.S. government must not only lie to the world, but must also lie (especially) to Americans. The image of a government scheming to deceive its people is further promoted by the claim that U.S. journalists were asking the appropriate questions, pursuing the truth, in the 007 incident, but were being resisted by an administration creating floods of gross slander. This understanding of the U.S. government—and its relationship with the American people—suggests a manipulative, conspiratorial form of administration. It explains U.S. foreign policy solely on the basis of a dominating elite who overwhelms an uninformed or impotent public.

While the images seem to parallel, to a great degree, the images Americans are presented of Soviet society, the degree of attention directed toward domination and the nature of that domination seem different. In the U.S. press there seem to be two different types of stories about the Soviet Union: the first, and most frequent, about the international threat the Soviet Union poses; the second, about the oppression experienced by the Soviet people themselves. While the two are certainly related, they seem most frequently to be treated separately, though the second issue lends to the threatening image of a massive Soviet Union that presents an immediate threat to the rest of the world. The Eastern press, at least in the case examined here, seems to have combined the presentation of the two issues—an internationally aggressive U.S. foreign policy and a repressive U.S. government. A well-intentioned people are misled and manipulated by a malevolent government. This contrasts significantly with a more passive and sullen Soviet population that—with the exception of notable dissidents—has been cowed into submission.

Granma clearly did not provide a variety of alternative perspectives and understandings in its accounts of the shooting of KAL Flight 007. Much as Americans have been led to believe, the Cuban newspaper presented a rather one-dimensional view of the world with the United States—or at least its government—as the force of evil and Soviet officials the source of truth. *Granma* presented a version of the shooting that was overwhelmingly critical of what it claimed to be U.S. participation and absolutely consistent with the Soviet version of reality—it could not avoid consistency with Soviet reality given its reliance on Soviet journalism.

It is interesting, however, to compare similarities in the presentations of the U.S. and Cuban presses. While it is important not to minimize the anomalies in American journalism—occasional critical articles, the work of Tom Wicker, the availability of alternative press such as the *Nation*—it is necessary to note also that while the principles guiding the journalism of the United States and Cuba are quite different, the journalistic products share some similar characteristics. In both cases the intentions and honesty of the favored government and its representatives were never doubted. Similarly, the worst intentions and motivations were consistently assumed of the other side. The assumptions about ourselves and our adversaries, or more fundamentally the identification with the appropriate side, whether it be the result of overt government control or the (not so subtle) influence of political culture, produce the same kind of jingoistic journalism. There are striking similarities here in the character—though obviously not the perspective—of the American free press and a state-controlled press. The free press of the United States is not legally or organizationally bound to the government in the manner of the Cuban press, yet its attitude toward its government was much the same as that of *Granma*, or more correctly *Tass*, toward the government of Cuba and its allies.

Though both presses possess a (competing) sense of national purpose, there are also most important differences between them. When it is political culture rather than government decree that shapes the work of journalists, there remains the (not insignificant) possibility of counter-cultural, counter-hegemonic journalism. The presence of some (though limited) variability within American journalism, along with the (unavoidably) lived and reported contradictions within the culture and the social system, make possible the imagination and the possible realization of alternative realities. The contradictions, of course, are not immediately experienced or reported as such, but instead as personal failings or glitches within an otherwise smoothly functioning and valued system. The experience, though, along with the limited critique available in the press, provide the seed and soil for the development of alternative social relations. The variability within American journalism, though quite limited, is not insignificant—t least in its potential.

REFERENCES

Schiller, Dan (1979) "An Historical Approach to Objectivity and Professionalism in American News Reporting," *Journal of Communication* 29: 46–57.
———. (1981) *Objectivity and the News: The Public and the Rise of Commercial Journalism* (Philadelphia: University of Pennsylvania Press).

4
SOLIDARITY

We have seen how the U.S. press, even in comparison to the (selected) press of Canada, provides a perspective that is exceptionally critical of the Soviet Union. Though American journalists had access to, and indeed knowledge of, information that could reduce the impression of Soviet culpability and avoid reinforcing the image of an immoral or amoral Soviet society, that information was consistently ignored or "hidden" within their work. Instead, the Soviet Union was painted in absolute and negative terms. The U.S. administration's self-serving explanations of events surrounding the destruction of Flight 007, in contrast, were accepted without reservation, despite acknowledged inadequacies. The comparison with the Canadian press has provided a (qualified) example of how the issues might have been alternatively presented.

Further examination of the American press will provide insight into the nature of its presentation of world events. Specifically, the press's presentation of the role of the Soviet Union in these events will be examined. By understanding the portrayal of the Soviet Union, its origins and meanings, we can further understand our political culture, which provides the frames used in the press's presentation of the world.

THE AMERICANIZATION OF SOLIDARITY

The second of the case studies considered in this work will examine news media coverage of the Polish labor union, Solidarity. To provide a context for this examination, a very brief summary of coverage of a 1970 strike of U.S. postal workers will be provided. While there are a great many fundamental differences in the nature of the strikes by the two unions, there are also significant similarities. Noting how specific aspects of the postal strike were presented will provide a source of comparison to better understand the presentation of events in Poland ten years later.

Of particular interest will be press support for the goals of the postal workers, press criticism for the workers' strike methods despite endorsement of the goals, press assignment of responsibility for the strike, press attention to the issue of economic disruption, and press concern for the issues of law and order. A comparison of coverage on these selected aspects of the two strikes will provide a basis on which a more detailed consideration of news media presentation of events in Poland can be accomplished.

A number of studies of industrial-labor relations news (Knight 1982; Glasgow Media Group 1980, 1982) have suggested that the way such news is presented serves to "draw upon and reproduce certain dominant assumptions and beliefs about the nature of social reality" (Knight 1982:61). These studies focused on media treatment of industrial relations within the nation of the news organizations considered. If the thesis that news accounts are shaped by and tend to reproduce hegemonic reality is to be supported, we should be able to understand accounts of workers' actions in other countries as originating in the dominant interests and values of the home society of the reporting news organizations. At the same time, comparison of accounts of industrial relations at home with accounts of relations abroad can provide insight into the specific content of the favored reality.

A comparison of selected aspects of news coverage of the events surrounding the early activities of Solidarity with parallel aspects of the earlier strike of American postal workers, followed by a more detailed examination of accounts in Poland, can serve as a challenge to the news-as-ideology thesis and potentially as an exercise that uses the assumptions of the thesis to identify further the hegemonic ideology. It will be shown below that selected basic features of the two strikes, though fundamentally comparable, were presented or framed in dissimilar manners. Such inconsistencies would appear to undermine the view of news simply as a mirror that provides an objective, untampered image of reality. It is not enough, though, for there to be inconsistencies in the presentation of news for the news-as-ideology thesis to be supported. The inconsistencies must be systematic and promoted or guided by an ideological perspective grounded in the social order within which the accounts originate. The apparent inconsistencies must be shown to be consistent with socially accepted assumptions that provide the basis for our understanding of reality. That is, the ideas shaping the framing of news accounts need to be shown to be dominant political ideas of a particular social and historical location. Consideration of the nature of the inconsistencies in media presentation, along with further examination of the accounts of Solidarity, will provide opportunities to identify more specifically the nature of the hegemonic view of the world that is the origin of the news frames utilized.

THE POSTAL STRIKE

Support for Cause

Although there is a place reserved in most newspapers and magazines, in the form of editorial and op-ed pages or columns, for opinion and perspectives, it is not unusual to find attitudes exhibited throughout the pages of "hard" news. Accounts, for example, of the financial situation of U.S. postal workers at the time of their 1970 strike seemed to indicate a genuine sympathy for the workers' plight.

At the time of the postal strike, the starting pay for postal workers was $6,176. After 20 years of service, the maximum a postal employee could earn was $8,442 (*NYT*, March 8:1; *Time*, March 30:11). Not all workers received the maximum even after 20 years with the post office (*NYT*, March 22:70). The media acknowledged the hardship experienced by the workers receiving such a salary. *Newsweek* (March 30:16), *Time* (March 30:12), and the *New York Times* (March 20:40) each had stories profiling "typical" postal workers and their economic plight. The profiles or human interest slant provided readers with an opportunity to understand and even identify with the workers' cause in a manner that the mere recitation of salary statistics could not accomplish. The situation of postal workers became personalized. Their difficulties could be understood on a level of individual struggle rather than labor–management/government conflict.

The *New York Times* story profiled a 49-year-old postman who had to work additional jobs to support his family. After 23 years as a letter carrier, the man earned $8,400 in a city where, it was reported, the federal government estimated that an income of $11,236 was required for a moderate standard of living for a family of four. The *Times* also reported a postal union estimate that at the current rate of pay, approximately 7 percent of its members received welfare assistance (March 18:94).

Initial reports described somewhat ambiguously the government's responsibility for the developments preceding the postal strike. The "suddenness" of the strike movement was identified as the reason that Congress and the administration were unable to respond promptly and effectively to the situation (*Time*, March 30:11). The "docile," "dependable men in grey" had never before "raised so much as a pinky in organized protest" (*Newsweek*, March 30:24; *Time*, March 30:11). *Newsweek*, however, acknowledged that "there have been ominous rumblings from the rank and file for many months in a four-way stalemate between the White House, the House Committee, the Senate Committee and the politically powerful postal unions" (*NYT*, March 20:40).[1] It was conceded, "even by the Post Office authorities," that the postal workers had been shortchanged in federal pay increases during the previous decade (*Newsweek*, March 30:15) and that the 41 percent pay increase that Congress had recently voted itself made the situation all the more volatile (*Time*, March 30:13).

The economic hardship experienced by the postal workers, along with the impression of an unwillingness on the part of the government to respond to the situation, provided an image sympathetic to the workers' plight. Such a sympathetic image, however, was not to suggest support for the strike itself. The cause may be reasonable and just, but the means chosen to advance that cause, as will be indicated below, were viewed as illegal, dangerous, and unjust.

Strike as Threat to Society

The strike, though motivated by legitimate concerns, was presented in the news as a "desperate rejection of the law" (*Newsweek*, March 30:15), leaving "Government's authority ... in question and the well-being of business, institutions and individuals in jeopardy" (*Time*, April 6:8). More than a simple inconvenience, the strike was a threat to society. On all levels, from the individual to the corporation to the state, the strike endangered health, if not survival itself.

Newsweek seemed to indicate a particular concern for the personal difficulties created by the strike. It was reported that the postal workers' refusal to report to their jobs, "tied up pay, pension and welfare checks, dividends, tax refunds, wedding invitations, medical prescriptions, Easter cards, stock proxies, Oscar ballots, census forms, alimony payments and passports..." (March 30:23). Families with sons and husbands in Vietnam seemed to make most apparent the hardship caused by the strike. It became impossible to send cookies to a son in Vietnam (*Newsweek*, March 30:16) or to receive a reassuring letter from a husband stationed there (*Newsweek*, March 19:52). It was lamented that "there was no estimating the minor and major individual tragedies caused by overdue dividend checks, costly medicines delayed by the strike and airline tickets that would arrive after the flight has departed" (*Newsweek*, March 30:17).

Estimates of the economic damage, both experienced and potential, resulting from the postal strike were a constant feature of the news accounts. The *Times* included daily reports of the economic crisis. A front-page headline in the paper on the first day of the strike read, "City's Economy Sapped by Strike" (March 19:1). The next day the headline on the front page reinforced the point: "City's Economy Worsens in 2nd Day of Postal Strike" (March 20:1). The same day another headline read, "Wall Street Fears a Shutdown if the Postal Strike Continues" (March 20:40). The following day a headline was "The Pinch Tightens on Business Here as Undelivered Letters and Parcels Pile Up" (March 21:12). Headlines describing or forecasting economic doom were a regular feature of reporting in the *Times*. As the next business week began, the headline of a story about the strike was "Industry Girds for Another Week of Mail Tie-Ups: National Guard Ready to Serve" (March 23:36). Despite efforts by the corporate community to overcome the crippling effects of the strike, it was unable to overcome the difficulties. Tuesday's headline told the reader, "Wall Street Using Copters and Cars to Move Necessary Mail, but Economy Lags" (March 24:34).

As indicated below, news accounts of Solidarity ten years later also noted the economic disruption caused by the striking workers. It, however, was not given attention of the same sort as the earlier American strike. It was not a primary focus or the subject of repeated headlines. When economic disruption was considered, it was usually discussed either in terms of an already weak Communist economy or as an indication of the strength of the strikers' resolve. Economic disruption was not a significant concern in reports of events in Poland except when it was used to highlight other issues that were the focus of the reports. Danger to the economy, though, was a primary concern that provided the frame for much of the reporting about the postal strike.

While accounts of the postal strike in both magazines and the *Times* catalogued personal hardships caused by the work stoppage, and indicated the economic dangers created by the strike, the most serious concern seemed to be the threat the strike presented to the government and the foundation of American society. This concern was shared among all three news outlets. At the end of the strike, *Time* reported that with

inflation ravaging the pocketbooks of virtually all Americans, it is hardly surprising that so many unions are seeking more money and backing up their demands with strike threats. What is surprising, however, is the new militance of federal employees, who are forbidden by law to strike. Public employees are now refusing to be bound by the legal structures that previously maintained discipline. (April 6:8)

The strike, the flagrant disregard for the laws of the land, and the indication of disregard for the welfare of the American people was clearly a concern indicated in the press. The strike represented or was seen to be symptomatic of a larger trend in society. The strike would lend support to the trend seen in the public to degrade or disregard its government and social institutions. The postal strike was understood to support and encourage the disrespect of those forces which provide order in our society. It was observed that the strike

underscores the helplessness of government in the face of organized, even if nonviolent, lawlessness. It also points up the growing tendency on the part of individuals and special interests to press their demands despite the havoc wrought in the community, and demonstrates the deterioration of discipline that has become a major challenge to U.S. society in recent years.... The Government's effectiveness—or lack of it—in halting the postal walkout could thus determine whether other federal employees decide that the way to a pay raise is through the picket lines. (*Time*, March 30:15)

Newsweek agreed that "beyond all the discomfort and dislocations, the walkouts put Federal antistrike laws to their first serious test in history—a test to the capacity of government to function" (April 6:33). The magazine included an article discussing all the possible consequences of the "Pandora's Box" which had been opened (April 6:25). The concern indicated in the news accounts clearly was not limited to the integrity of federal antistrike laws and the possibility of strikes by other federal workers. Rather, the concern was for the symbolic and actual loss of respect and even tolerance of the previously valued institutions and laws of American society. The concerns expressed in the press corresponded to those of President Nixon, who, during the strike, warned, "What is at issue is the survival of a government based upon law" (*Newsweek*, April 6:33).

It was not, though, simply the principle of constitutional government that was of value, but instead a particular government (that of the United States) and particular law (that of the United States) that was of supreme value. In the case of other governments and the law of other lands, the value of their survival depends, as will be indicated below in the discussion of news coverage of Solidarity, upon how the news media understand their contribution to American interest, and the media's definition of that interest.

Finally, responsibility for the inability to reach a settlement in the postal strike was put squarely, in the news accounts, on the workers. The *Times* reported, for example, when the postal workers rejected an agreement made between the postal unions and the federal government that "All over the country postal workers were rejecting the agreement in Washington Friday between leaders of seven postal unions and the Nixon administration" (March 22:1). The responsibility for the situation was placed with the striking postal workers. If the *Times* had instead reported that the union and government had still failed to meet the expressed needs of the workers, the inferred responsibility would have been placed differently. The *Times*, in its manner of reporting, was assigning the responsibility for the continued strike on the postal workers for their rejection of the accord rather than on the union and government for the quality of the offer.

The placement of responsibility or, as implied in this case, fault, is particularly interesting when compared with developments in Poland a decade later. In the case of Poland, at least initially, it was said to be the inability or unwillingness of the government to respond appropriately to the strikers—not the actions of the strikers—which perpetuated the difficulties. Responsibility for the failure of the Polish government and Solidarity to reach accords was placed on an unresponsive and intransigent government. In neither of the cases did the media simply report an inability of the contending parties to reach an accord. In each case a particular party is identified as being particularly contentious. At least on the basis of supporting evidence provided in the news reports, the assignment of belligerence seems to be grounded more in political perspective than in the stances of the respective parties.

THE SOLIDARITY MOVEMENT

Religious and Disciplined

It is a common impression of the Solidarity movement in Poland, that it was greatly influenced by the participants' religious background and a commitment, both practical and ethical, to the avoidance of violence. Religion is an element which was consistently noted in descriptions of individuals and groups of workers. It was understood as a source of motivation and inspiration as well as an important factor in the maintenance of discipline. It was observed that "If solidarity was one of the strikers' strengths, so was their shared religiosity" (*Time*, September 8:31). Solidarity demonstrations were frequently described in terms of religious activity and symbolism. Crowds of demonstrators were described, for example, as "thousands of strikers and their families kneeling at the gates of the shipyard, praying and singing hymns before the flower-bedecked portrait of a Polish Pope" (*Time*, September 1:20). Photographs of workers kneeling in prayer were common in the media reports (for example, *Newsweek*, September 8:31; *Time*, September 1:22). Photos often showed the gate of the Gdansk shipyard with its grillwork "ornamented with pictures of the Virgin Mary and color portraits of the Pope..." (*Time*, September 1:25). It was observed that the gate looked "like a religious shrine overflowing with votive offerings" (*NYT*, August 25:1).

Shared religious conviction seemed to define Solidarity's purpose and manner. The movement's commitment and discipline were consistent features of news reports. Perhaps the best examples of discipline and order came out of the occupied Lenin Shipyard, called the "Gdansk Commune" by Paul Martin, the *Newsweek* reporter who visited the shipyard. The *New York Times* and *Time* also had reporters at the shipyard. "Morale was astonishingly high.... Many of the strikers were passionately religious ... the strike committee issues calls for caution" (*Newsweek*, September 1:28–29). It apparently was seen as significant, an indication of the workers' determination and self-control, that alcohol was banned within the shipyard. Martin made note of it in his report, and *Time* titled its article about the occupied shipyard, "Fervent Unity, and a Ban on Vodka" (September 8:31). The unity and organization found at the shipyard also impressed the reporter from the *Times*. He found that "The strike committee has spawned a sizable apparatus for administration ... guards ... crowd control monitors ... couriers ... donations committee ... food committee ... press center, complete with translators for the growing crops of foreign journalists" (September 28:8). Solidarity was apparently prepared to meet the challenges of the task at hand.

The shipyard was a place organized to maintain discipline and function effectively. Such organization, combined with the talents and skills of union leadership, suggested reason for hope in the workers' struggle. It was noted how "remarkable was the display of discipline, organization and shrewd negotiating skills provided by the Gdansk-based Interfactory Strike Committee" (*Time*, September 15:33). Political observers apparently agreed. A West German Chancellory expert was quoted as marvelling that "The amazing thing about the strikers is not only their incredible discipline and excellent organization, but also their leaders' shrewdness and sophisticated negotiating tactics" (*Time*, September 8:33). Union membership also recognized and were apparently quite proud of their self-discipline and singleness of effort. A shipyard foreman observed,

"Nobody is misbehaving. This is no time for fun. We're all in this together" (*Time*, September 1:26).

Loss of Discipline

The images presented in the media consistently portrayed a movement of courageous, responsible workers supported by the mass of Polish people. The commitment and enthusiasm of the workers was restrained only by their self-discipline. Such observations make it all the more interesting when, in December, it began to be noted that "Lech Walesa, the Solidarity leader, has had increased difficulty controlling his unruly rank and file" (*Time*, December 15:42). It was during December that reports began to indicate that the strikers had suddenly lost their sense of restraint and instead seemed intent on provoking a dangerous confrontation. Only during December, the last month of accounts that were analyzed, are signs of incaution on the part of the workers highlighted. Earlier reports indicated a movement of workers who were, while brave, also cautious and responsible. Walesa was quoted during the first week of December as warning union members that "It will be a great mess if we go on strike.... Let us not forget that the tanks and rockets could be the reply." The reader was advised that this was "an unmistakable warning about the ominous possibility of Soviet intervention" (*Time*, December 8:46). On the same page, the reader was told that "Polish workers are strangely nonchalant about the possibility of Soviet intervention." Also on the page is the assessment of a "West German analyst" who observed, "By what they do and say, you would think that many of these fellows deliberately want to tweak the bear's nose." According to a "concerned analyst in Bonn," "The Poles seem to have a particular talent for courting national suicide" (*Time*, December 22:36). These Poles hardly seem recognizable as the same people who just a short time ago had displayed remarkable discipline, organization, and shrewd negotiating skills.

This pattern of reporting is particularly evident in the two news magazines. Toward the end of the year, there were significant changes in the nature of the accounts that appeared in the *Times*, but these changes were more in the nature of the direction of focus rather than a redefinition of the participants. Consideration of changes in reporting in the *Times* will be treated in the section of this chapter that examines media treatment of the possibility of Soviet military intervention in Poland.

Union Leadership

The change in the image presented of the movement rank and file corresponded to the change in the image presented of their leadership. Movement leadership, and particularly Lech Walesa, received a great deal of attention in the media. Early reports observed that "The charismatic Walesa, 37, has emerged as a national hero who can mobilize hundreds of thousands of workers" (*Time*,

November 3:57). Walesa was described as "the workingmen's hero" (*Time*, September 15:33), "a national folk hero" (*Time*, October 6:51), and "an authentic hero" (*Time*, September 8:33). He was a "Polish folk hero and a world figure" (*Newsweek*, December 8:42), a "master gamesman" (*Newsweek*, December 8:40) and an "adroit politician" (*Newsweek*, December 8:42). Despite all the adulation and fervent attention he received, Walesa was still able to maintain his reason. An article in the *Times* about Walesa was headlined, "Leader of Strike Knows the Season for Talking" (*NYT*, August 31:16).

Photographs helped provide readers with an image of Solidarity's leader. Articles about Walesa were often accompanied by photographs that depicted him as a religious family man. An article about him in *Newsweek* included a photo of Walesa with a daughter. There was a picture of the Pope on a wall in the background. Another photo on the same page showed Walesa at the stove with his children around him (December 8:42). The text of earlier articles would have led the reader to expect Walesa's religious commitment, having described him, for example, as "a fervently religious man" who regularly confers with the local Cardinal during negotiations (*Newsweek*, November 24:75). Articles presented a consistent image. Walesa was seen as a family man devoted to his six children. He was not conceited, but it was acknowledged that he did sometimes exhibit a "puckish cockiness." He was a man of dignity who expected the same of others (*Time*, September 8:33).

In contrast to the earlier impressions, by December it was being observed that "it has taken all of Walesa's guile, humor and an occasional flash of old fashioned demagoguery to hold that volatile union together" (*Newsweek*, December 8:40). A short time earlier, the union was remarkable in its self-discipline and order, and Walesa was charismatic and able to mobilize hundreds of thousands of workers. Suddenly, "He teases and even browbeats the rank and file into line." Journalists seem to have discovered a new Walesa, very much unlike the old one. "Some observers detect in him a touch of demagoguery and personal vanity. ... In interviews, he sometimes seems flippant to the point of arrogance. ... [H]e can be remarkably high-handed while chairing union meetings, often interrupting speakers in mid-sentence and imposing his own views" (*Time*, Dececember 29:31).

The Polish Government

As the presentation of Solidarity and its leadership changed quite dramatically during the last month of 1980, so did that of the Polish government. The initial response of the government to the strike of the Polish workers was a refusal to negotiate. In *Newsweek* it was explained that the government's refusal was prompted by its own weakness. It was suggested that to engage in talks with the strikers would further undermine its already weakened authority (August 25:21).

The picture of a weak, intimidated government was commonly presented early in the strike. The Polish government, when it did engage in negotiations, was reported to have "caved in" rather than to have compromised on points of contention (*Newsweek*, August 25:46). When the government did compromise it was described as a "humbling strategy of compromise" (*Newsweek*, September 8:30). If Gierek's government had caved in and been humbled it might have been because as "the atmosphere of crisis deepened in official Communist Party circles in Poland.... [T]he leadership was apparently unable to make key decisions on what to offer the striking workers" (*NYT*, August 30:11). A headline in the *New York Times* described the situation: "Vacillation in Warsaw: Government Uncertain How to Negotiate with Strikers" (August 10:4). Apparently, as the government was losing its authority over the nation, it also found itself internally without leadership and direction. The lack of a clear response to the situation on the part of the government could introduce the possibility of a general strike. Such a strike, one official said, would be due to the leadership's indecisiveness but would be blamed on the workers.

Readers were repeatedly reminded of the earlier government responses to worker activity. While Gierek was reported to be "forbidding strong-arm tactics" (*Newsweek*, August 18:40), it was noted that similar protests in 1970 had brought down the government of Wladyslaw Gomulka. "The precipitating cause then was that the troops opened fire on strikers, killing scores of them" (*NYT*, August 20:1). It must have been only a bit reassuring to readers then when they were informed that "Apart from flying and trucking reinforcements into the Baltic area, Gierek made no show of armed force. Instead he appealed for reason and moderation in a 25 minute radio and television address to the nation" (*Time*, September 1:40). The magazines, like the *Times*, featured regular reminders of the government's bloody response to earlier strikes. Any note of the government's current position of moderation was frequently followed by recollections that ten years earlier "the government's brutal response left hundreds of workers dead" (*Time*, August 25:40), and that "Ten years ago, the government used force to halt strikes in the Baltic ports against high food prices. The ensuing bloodshed—hundreds of workers were killed—led to the downfall of Party Chief Wladyslaw Gomulka" (*Time*, August 4:40).

The Gierek government was reported to be a bit more cautious than earlier administrations, but the reports were often qualified. "So far at least, the authorities have gone out of their way to play down the threat of force" (*NYT*, August 20:10). On the same page that this statement appeared were also rumors of the government "moving to break the strike with force." While a government spokesperson reported "no information on troop movements" and denied that there was any plan to dislodge strikers by force, KOR leader Kuron was being quoted as telling journalists that "militia troops have been observed moving toward Gdansk." The government denial was followed by another reminder of earlier violence.

While there is an initial appearance in these reports of providing a balanced account with the use of government and dissident sources, the sequence of quotes and the repeated reminder of past violence would lead the reader to believe that a government-provoked violent confrontation was at least likely if not inevitable. The constant reference to past violence, the portrayal of a desperate government, and dissident reports of troop movements suggest that the government spokesperson might be a bit suspect.

By the end of the year, media portrayal of the government, like that of Solidarity, had rather suddenly undergone great changes. An indication of these changes is the dramatic revision in the assessment of Polish Communist Party Chief Stanislaw Kania. "Kania has moved aggressively to rid the party of officials who are corrupt, incompetent or tainted by past associations with the Gierek regime" (*Time*, December 29:26). Three months earlier, Kania had been introduced to the readers of *Time* as "a loyal apparatchnik with orthodox views and no inclination to buck Moscow . . . the few Westerners who have met him have been struck by his shrewdness and tough-mindedness, as well as his utter lack of humor . . . the Kremlin's creature." The same article included the observation of a "West German specialist" who noted Kania "has the strong ambition and ruthlessness needed to survive at the top levels" (September 15:34). In an unusual acknowledgment that its characterization of a participant in the developments in Poland had substantially changed, *Time* reported that Kania had "surprised Western analysts with his moderation and political acumen. In public, he is softspoken and low-key, despite his burly bulldog looks. Kania has made the unions work hard for every concession, but for the most part he has avoided slashing rhetoric and underhanded tactics" (December 29:26).

In a period of three months (actually during one month, December) Kania was transformed from a humorless "creature" to a soft-spoken, politically insightful moderate. One might wonder about the origins of this dramatic transformation. Had Kania become a new man, or had media presentation of the man—along with presentation of other elements of the "story"—changed as new news frames, or defining assumptions of events, were substituted for old ones? If there has been a substitution of news frames, how can we explain the change?

Soviet Invasion Scenarios

The increased criticism in the news magazines of Solidarity and its leadership near the end of 1980 was developing at the same time that representation of the Polish government was becoming more favorable. As there appeared no dramatic changes in the position of either Solidarity or the government at this period, we must look for another explanation for the change in reporting. It seems clear that these changes accompanied an increased concern about the involvement of the Soviet Union in the Polish situation. Certainly, news accounts reminded readers of the Soviet threat throughout coverage of events in Poland, but there was a dramatic increase in this aspect of the coverage beginning in late November and early December. *Newsweek*'s cover story of December 8 was of the "Challenge to Moscow." A headline in the same issue reported "Moscow's Polish Crisis" (December 8:40). The magazine's cover the next week declared, "Poland: The Invasion Threat." The issue included a photograph with the caption, "Warsaw Pact maneuvers: Moscow's threat of fraternal support" (December 8:39). It also included a story entitled, "How Moscow Would Invade," with a map of an "invasion scenario" (December 8:40). The following week *Time* reported a "possible invasion scenario" suggested by "experts in Bonn" (December 15:43). Following this report was a discussion of possible U.S. responses. The next issue of the magazine reported that "U.S. intelligence experts in Washington believe that the Kremlin will sooner or later have to use force in Poland. The likelihood of invasion will remain high, they say, even if the recent Soviet military buildup turns out to be a bluff" (December 22:36). This issue also reported the locations, numbers, and activities of Soviet troops and suggested possible NATO responses (December 22:37).

The change in the news magazines' portrayal of the participants in Poland and the increased attention to the likelihood of Soviet military intervention occurred at the same time. This cannot be explained simply as a coincidence. Instead, as will be discussed below with specific reference to the coverage of the *Times*, an American preoccupation with the Soviet Union and the symbolic significance of that nation—which was in large part responsible for the initial assumptions used to frame the reports of events in Poland—required a reinterpretation of the participating parties when developments introduced an increased possibility of an expansion of Soviet influence and power rather than a public rejection of Communist authority within the Soviet sphere. Before discussing the origins of the change of frames used to report the events surrounding the activities of Solidarity, another example of the changes in the nature of news coverage will be cited.

The *Times* Change of News Frame

It was noted above that in the case of the *New York Times*, it was primarily a redirection of focus rather than a redefinition of the participants that characterized the change in reports about Poland during the last month of 1980. That redirection was consistent with the news magazines' attention to the issue of Soviet military intervention. The *Times*, however, rather than presenting images of Solidarity and the Polish government that were dramatically changed over time, seemed to become less attentive to these contending forces as their importance was being eclipsed by developing events. Toward the end of November articles about events in Poland became increasingly few as articles focusing on the possibility of Soviet military intervention became increasingly frequent. While it seems that the portrayal of Solidarity remained rather consistent over time and that the Polish government, though presented as being increasingly nonconfrontative later in the year, did not experience as extreme a change as was indicated in the magazines, it is difficult to make strong generalizations about the consistency of imagery because of the limited direct attention given the two parties.

In the *Times*, as in the news magazines, the possibility that Solidarity's confrontation with Polish authorities might provoke military intervention by the Soviet Union was repeatedly noted. The possibility was communicated directly and by reference to past incursions such as that into Czechoslovakia in 1968. It was not an obvious reversal of past reporting then when the newspaper began to pay increasing attention to the issue of a Soviet military threat. While not a complete reversal, the change does represent a significant alteration in the characterization of events in Poland. Though accomplished in a manner different from that of the news magazines, and achieved a bit more subtly, the *Times* transformed its presentation of the Solidarity movement, from a heroic effort of the people of Poland to improve their lives and expand their freedoms against the existing limits of a Warsaw Pact nation under Soviet domination, to an opportunity for the Soviet Union to reinforce its grip on Eastern Europe and thereby increase its capabilities of world influence. The manner in which this was done can be observed by looking at the change in coverage of Poland during the last months of the year.

Initially, the *Times* presentation of events and participants was quite similar to that of the news magazines. References to the Soviet Union were similar also, though possibly proportionally a bit less frequent. During October, for example, reference to the Soviet Union did not play a dominant role in determining coverage. In the middle of the month, it was reported that East German leader Erich Honecker had warned of possible action by other Warsaw Pact nations if required to respond to a threat to communism in Poland. The article, though, is not alarmist and apparently the editors did not believe that it merited front-page presentation (October 15:7). Five days later a short article announced that Soviet Foreign Minister Andrei Gromyko had arrived in Poland, but it was explained that he was attending a regularly scheduled meeting of Warsaw Pact Foreign Ministers (October 20:3). The following day, in reference to efforts by the Polish government to assert its authority after having made some concessions to strikers, it was reported that the government was attempting "to mollify other Communist countries. In recent days, East Germany, Czechoslovakia, Rumania and the Soviet Union have all criticized developments in Poland and warned against 'anti-socialist elements' gaining too much power" (October 21:3). The possibility of intervention is suggested in the article, but the issue of Soviet intervention does not yet prevent the notice or exclude consideration of other aspects of developments in Poland.

The Possible Soviet Invasion

An article of October 30 illustrates a pattern of reporting that was to become predominant in the *Times*. Though treatment of news from Poland was not yet exclusively and continuously concerned with the Soviet Union, the article does focus on Polish–Soviet relations and provides a maybe-they-will-maybe-they-won't approach that will become characteristic of news stories in the *Times*. In a variant of the on-the-one-hand-on-the-other-hand style of reporting that is intended to conform to the requirements of objectivity that assume there are two sides to every story, the *Times* at the same time alarmed the reader with a report that a Soviet invasion of Poland was imminent and suggested that such an invasion was not likely—at least not immediately. The article, referring to a meeting between Polish and Soviet government leaders that was held in Moscow, was headlined "Top Polish Leaders Fly to Soviet Today" and carried the subhead "Purpose of Sudden Trip is Unclear but Sharp Talks are Expected on Free Union Demands." These headlines give the clear impression that Polish leaders are ultimately answerable to Moscow. The second paragraph reinforces this understanding dramatically when reference is made to a similar meeting with Czechoslovakian leaders prior to the invasion by Soviet bloc troops in 1968. At the conclusion of the article, after having indicated alarm, it is reported that "According to Western diplomats with access to Soviet thinking, the prevailing feeling here is that the political struggle in Poland, though fraught with danger, is still in an early stage and that Polish leadership still has large reserves of power and influence to bring to bear" (October 30:6). The clear suggestion is that Moscow expects Polish authorities to be able to resolve the difficulties internally. The article was written by the *Times* Moscow correspondent, Anthony Austin.

A short article by the *Times* correspondent in Poland, John Darnton, who was to receive a Pulitzer Prize for his reporting, followed the longer article by Austin. Darnton, while also noting the tension of the situation, reported that Western diplomats saw the meeting as an "appropriate" visit of a new Polish leader to Moscow. Kania had assumed office less than two months earlier.

If a reader were to read only the headline and opening paragraphs of the first article, an understanding of almost absolute Soviet domination and an expectation of Soviet military intervention would be the reasonable result. If the reader were to read both articles more fully, confusion might be the understandable result. The presentation of two conflicting analyses was to become a pattern in the reporting of the *Times*. There were also headlines and opening paragraphs of an alarmist tone. The latter pattern, along with the development of an almost exclusive concern not with contestation and negotiation between Solidarity and the government, but with the issue of Soviet invasion, negates any possibility that the former pattern would satisfy the demands of objectivity or detached reporting. Like earlier reporting of events in Poland, reports later in the year were framed by an anti-socialist, anti-Soviet, American political culture. But the development of events as the year progressed required a redefinition of the situation to satisfy the demands of the hegemonic culture.

The Imminent Soviet Invasion

Throughout November the pattern of reporting in the *Times* continued and intensified until the beginning of December, when it was most extreme. An early

November report in the *Times* is of particular interest. The article, by Darnton, was headlined "After Heady Days of Strike, Poland Turns Gloomy" (November 6:2). The headline seems to describe the *Times* reporting style as well as Darnton's characterization of Poland. He reported that the economy had worsened, that there was no union–party relationship that had developed, and that relations with neighboring Communist nations continued to worsen. An increased number of Poles had applied for passports to the West. A "mother of two" was quoted as explaining that passport applications were in case "the tanks came." Again, the reader was given what appeared to be contradictory impressions. Darnton first reported that "The visit last week to Moscow by Stanislaw Kania, the new party leader, in which he obtained the Kremlin's public backing for his handling of the crisis so far, has temporarily dulled fears but has not dispelled them." Seven paragraphs later he reported, "The ominous official comments from Czechoslovakia and East Germany are read here as direct threats of intervention and they have not abated since Kania's trip to Moscow." The paragraphs between these two statements include numerous quotes that suggest that fear, at least among some Poles, has been neither dulled nor dispelled. A "highly respected Polish commentator" observed, "based on years of close observation, that what is developing will ultimately be unacceptable to the Soviet Union." A truck driver noted, "Everyone knows what it'll mean if the Russians come. The situation is so bad we've got no choice. Let them come, we'll fight." An elderly housekeeper, remembering World War II, "sighed," "Oh, Russian soldiers, you have no idea what they are like." An historian, also recalling the war, observed, "The chances for intervention are greater than they've ever been. And then what? A national hunger strike? A few people in the forests with guns? We'll be abandoned by the West again, just as we were in 1939."

Darnton has, in his article, at least nominally given the appearance of providing alternative assessments of the invasion possibility. But the tenor of the article, particularly his use of quotes from Poles "on the street," communicates the likelihood of invasion. The quotes of "regular people" as opposed to the more usual "knowledgeable Western official" or "Bonn Chancellory expert" leave a lasting impression. The imagery provoked by the elderly housekeeper or the historian recalling the past abandonment by the West is powerful. The article illustrates how reporting in the *Times* was becoming preoccupied with concern about a Soviet invasion. No longer, it seems, were Poles asked about their goals and dreams. They were instead asked about their fears. This was so even at a time when Darnton himself had reported that those fears had been dulled. One might wonder whose fears are most illustrated in the report, those of Poles, or those of American journalists?

Articles about Poland during the rest of the month continued to focus on the possibility of invasion. For a while the articles noted joint Soviet–Polish military maneuvers (for example, November 9:6) and continued concern in the Soviet Union due to wildcat strikes that suggested Solidarity's leadership was unable to control the rank and file (for example, November 17:12).

Later in the month it was reported that "Soviet Ends Activity Near Poland"

(November 18:12) and "Russian Move Into Poland Held Remote" (November 24:3). The November 24 article began with the by then characteristic ambiguousness: "The threat of armed Soviet intervention in Poland has receded in recent days, but Western diplomats and analysts doubt that it has disappeared." It is next observed that

In public, Soviet officials, like the controlled newspapers, are extremely critical of the independent trade union movement, sometimes so critical that they seem to be laying the groundwork for military action. But in private conversations, another picture emerges. Kremlin policy-makers voice concern in their talks with Westerners, but they say they hope and believe that the Polish government is in control.

Despite these private assurances, the author of the article, R. W. Apple, Jr., suggests that the Soviet announcements are aimed at two audiences. "The Soviet leadership seems to be telling the Poles that there is a limit to the Kremlin's tolerance and to be preparing a case for intervention in the minds of the Soviet people in case it should be needed."

Duplicating Washington's Frame

The ambiguity of the message communicated by the *Times* seems similar to the ambiguous messages of the U.S. government reported in the newspaper later in the month. In an article headlined "U.S., Worried, Hopes for Calm in Poland," and subheaded "Washington Aides Voice Concern—State Department Advises Attitude of Moderation" (November 27:11), a series of observations by U.S. government officials failed to clarify the situation any more than the media had.

Criticism of journalists for their reliance on government sources is given strong support here, as such reliance makes the article almost incomprehensible. The suggestion is not that government controls the news or has journalists "in its hip pocket." There is, instead, a question whether political assumptions—founded in a common culture—should provide common preoccupations, which, in turn, intensify those assumptions. Further, the shared assumptions discourage journalistic skepticism beyond accepted bounds of "reasonable" political discussion. At times of "crisis" it becomes particularly unlikely that these bounds will be violated and government representatives or prevailing political interpretations will be challenged. Once the sense of crisis is shared, the cultural forces encouraging further shared perceptions are intensified.

A common preoccupation with the Soviet Union made it more likely that a sense of crisis would develop when confronted with the possibility of Soviet influence in Poland. The sense of crisis then made it less likely that officials would be asked to support, or even make sense of, announcements such as those that appeared in the November 27 article.

The article began by noting that senior government officials indicated that they were "quite concerned" about the "tense situation in Poland." It was reported that "officials expressed apprehension about the possibility that continued demands by the workers might provoke a military crackdown by Polish or Soviet forces." The political situation in Poland appeared to be in "disarray" and there was growing speculation "that Stanislaw Kania might be replaced by a more authoritarian Communist Party leader; and that Soviet restraint was being sorely tested by the union, whose political demands seem to be making it a rival to the party." Against this background, the State Department's John H. Trather was quoted as saying, "We don't see any evidence that any Soviet troop action is imminent." Following this, he was quoted again, this time saying that the Soviets had recently moved "to improve the readiness of their forces in the area." An invasion, then, was not imminent but the forces were prepared and ready.

Admittedly, understanding of international relations requires an appreciation of subtlety, but there is also a difference between subtlety and obfuscation. The issue remained murky when it was reported in one paragraph that "officials said that Soviet forces along the border with Poland had conducted maneuvers and that armored equipment had been fueled and kept more ready than usual," and in the next paragraph that "American officials believe that the Soviet Union is showing restraint. . . . For the moment, one official said, the United States expects the Soviet Union to avoid direct involvement in Poland." The pattern of maybe-they-will-and-maybe-they-won't reporting that started earlier was still apparent at the end of November. Government pronouncements by Washington officials lent themselves to the continuation of this pattern and the cycle of mutual reinforcement among culture, journalism, and government.

The Completed Framing

The redirection of the *Times* coverage from an admired social movement toward a situation that threatened the balance of world power was complete by the beginning of December. Reports at the beginning of the month indicated both the moderating efforts of the Polish government and the increasing tension regarding Soviet intervention. For the first time, Kania was linking the union with hostile forces abroad, "but he pointedly omitted the national union leadership from his attack" (December 2:11). At the same time, the reader was informed in a headline, "Polish Border Zone Closed" (December 2:11). The closure of an area along the Polish–East German border "could be related to Warsaw Pact exercises and to Soviet contingency planning in case the Polish labor crisis worsens."

The following day the *Times* reported a shake-up within the Polish administration. The government changes, the report suggests, will permit Kania to manage more effectively the difficult situation. His hand will be strengthened "in advocating a tightrope course of cooperating with the independent union but attempting to curb labor unrest and demands for mere political concessions" (December 3:1). Another article on the front page was headlined, "U.S. Cautioning on Intervention in Polish Crisis." A White House statement warned against intervention in the Polish situation by outside forces, and officials said that intelligence reports were showing increased activity by Polish internal security forces. The article then notes that while the internal security forces had been used in 1970 and "on a smaller scale" in 1976, Polish authorities had avoided mobilizing the forces during the course of the current turmoil. An effort was being made to avoid violent confrontation. "The recommendation to avoid bloodshed this time was said by the Polish authorities to have come from Mr. Kania himself" (December 3:7). The article then returned to the primary theme.

As for the potential for intervention by the Soviet Union together with one or more of its allies, administration officials have not ruled out the possibility. However, an intelligence official said that, even though Soviet troops along the Polish frontiers were placed on a higher alert status last month, they were still "not positioned to move within an hour."

Just how likely was a Soviet invasion? In the final paragraph of the article, it is reported that another government official "said the reports about Soviet mobilization had been overstated in the press and that the situation was likely to end with a 'compromise on law and order' in Poland."

Aside from the issue of responsibility for the overstatements, a more immediate matter is apparent. Why does the headline of the article in which this quote appears, along with much of the first part of the article, suggest the likelihood of invasion? Further, why, in the same issue of the newspaper, are other stories headlined, "Rumanian Official Consults Brezhnev" (subhead: "Quick Mission of Foreign Ministers Adds More Speculation About Intention Toward Poland") (December 3:6), "Common Market Warns Russians Not to Take Action Against Poland" (December 3:8), and, noting again a development that had been reported the previous day, "German–Polish Zone Closed" (December 3:6). (The December 2 article about the restricted border area was attributed to Reuters; the December 3 article was "Special to *Times*.")

Interestingly, the article about the Rumanian Foreign Minister's visit to Moscow, written by R. W. Apple, Jr., acknowledges the confusion among journalists regarding the matter of Soviet intervention. Apple reported that "Moscow is filled with rumors, guesses and diplomatic analyses of the situation. Every reception and every dinner produces new material about the supposed imminence of Soviet military intervention in Poland." He further noted that "mobilization of certain Soviet troops caused spasms of speculation in the foreign community, where official information is often unobtainable and rumors are sometimes the only warning of foreign policy developments." The suggestion is that reliable information is difficult, or impossible, to obtain and there is instead reliance on rumor—an interesting suggestion by a journalist.

It is clear which rumors dominate reports. It is most interesting and telling to note, given the acknowledged scarcity of definitive sources, the journalistic attitude toward specific sources. Apple reported that "A check of a half-dozen Western military attaches produced nothing closer to a confirmation than the comment: 'It's possible but we know nothing.' " He then acknowledged that "A spokesman for the Soviet Foreign Ministry, in an unusually categorical denial, said it 'rejects all these rumors.' "

Clearly it was the noncommittal and ambiguous response of the Western military attaches that defined the situation for journalists rather than the categorical statement of the Soviet Foreign Ministry. It was assumed that in the refusal to make a definitive statement, the military attaches were communicating a purposeful message—a message passed on in the headlines and articles of the *Times*—while the certainty of the Soviet statement was an intentional effort to mislead. Why are not both sources treated equally critically?

The treatment indicates a predispositional journalistic attitude toward sources that is consistent with dominant political attitudes of our culture. Immediately below the article by Apple was placed the article of the closing of the German–Polish border area. It was reported that the border restrictions were "believed to be linked to trouble in Poland." The implication, given the context, is that military activities are taking place in the region in preparation for invasion. The intended but hidden message attributed to U.S. officials was bolstered, the categorical message of the Soviet official was denied.

Over the next week, attention to the possibility of Soviet invasion dominated the pages of the *Times*. Headlines during this time included, "Carter Expresses Concern of U.S. on Soviet Union" (subhead: " 'Unprecedented Buildup' on Polish Border is Cited") (December 4:1), "Polish Aide Won't Rule Out Report of Soviet Troops" (December 5:1), "U.S. Won't Exploit Crisis in Poland, Soviet Is Told" (December 5:14), "In East Berlin Poland Is Called Out of Control" (December 5:15), "Soviet Bloc Nations Meet Unexpectedly on Crisis in Poland" (December 6:1), "Polish Winter, Prague Spring: Does Kremlin See a Difference?" (December 7:4;1), "Russians Are Ready for Possible Move on Poland, U.S. Says" (December 8:1), "Moscow and Allies Activate Reserves: Invasion Fear Rises" (December 9:1), "Muskie Requesting Approval of Allies for Plan on Poland" (December 10:1), "Russian Forces Around Poland Termed Ready" (December 10:10), "U.S. to Supply NATO With Radar Planes" (subhead: "Request Arose from Possibility of Attack on Western Europe if Soviet Moves on Poland") (December 10:11). Headlines daily warned of the Soviet invasion of Poland, and by the end of the seven-day period the possibility of an invasion of Western Europe was being reported.

It might be suggested that the headlines within the *Times* were simply reflecting, or more accurately, reporting, the statements of the U.S. administration. The administration then, not the *Times*, was responsible for the sense of alarm communicated and promoted by the headlines. Such a suggestion, though, fails to account for the muted treatment given conflicting statements from administration sources. It also fails to explain the almost total monopolization of Poland-related articles by invasion concerns. Concern about the possible invasion does not necessitate the exclusion of information about developments in the efforts of Solidarity and the Polish workers.

During the period from December 5 to December 11, the pages of the *Times* included 23 articles focused primarily on the possible Soviet invasion and only four articles devoted to internal developments within Poland (see Appendix A). The four articles about events within Poland typically included reference to the invasion threat, and one was fully devoted to a report in the Polish Army newspaper that warned that union activity against the Communist system would not be tolerated.

The period immediately prior and subsequent to this seven-day period showed a similar ratio of invasion stories to Poland stories. Again, the overwhelming attention to the perceived invasion threat had served to redefine the Polish situation. Conflicts between Polish workers, Solidarity, and the Polish government still remained unresolved. While significant compromises had been worked out, issues important to each of the parties were still debated. Yet the *Times* attended little to these matters. The Polish situation had been redefined. The future of Western Europe was seen to be at risk. Polish interests, which had been seen as news that was fit to print, was fit no longer. American concerns and preoccupations were shaping the interpretation of events surrounding the developments in Poland, and that interpretation was then shaping the American understanding of internal Polish matters. Those internal matters that had merited front-page attention were disappearing from the newspaper altogether. These matters, as far as the *Times* was concerned, ceased to exist.

A Not Quite Seamless Hegemony

Reports during this time continued the earlier pattern of communicating alarm while including tempered acknowledgments that the possibility of invasion might be overstated. An article by Bernard Gwertzman (*NYT*, December 5:14) was one indication that at least some journalists seemed to appreciate the ambiguity and confusion of the situation. But it was not clear that there was an appreciation of the manner in which the news media fueled the alarm by minimizing—or making manageable—the confusion.

The day (December 4:1) before the article appeared, Gwertzman had authored an article reporting President Carter's statement of concern regarding the "unprecedented buildup" of Soviet forces along the Polish border. The article's headline and subhead noted Carter's concern and the buildup. Gwertzman had included in the first article a qualification of Carter's statement by a White House official who acknowledged that "there was still no evidence that Moscow had decided to intervene militarily." The official then qualified his qualification, adding that the statement by the President would not have been made unless Soviet intervention was viewed as a possibility. This article appeared on the first page of the *Times*.

In his article of the next day, which appeared on page 14, Gwertzman directly acknowledged the confusing and often contradictory messages that the administration was communicating. In the eighth paragraph of the piece, Gwertzman seems to suggest skepticism on the part of his colleagues and himself.

Yesterday Mr. Carter expressed "growing concern" over what he called "the unprecedented buildup" of Soviet forces along the Polish border. Today Mr. Brzezinski and other officials were pressed by reporters to explain what was "unprecedented" about it. There was some confusion in Washington, in fact, on the gravity of significance of Soviet military moves.

In the next paragraph Gwertzman provided a quote from National Security Adviser Brzezinski, defending the original buildup statement. But the following paragraphs indicate and promote skepticism toward Carter's statement and Brzezinski's defense.

Some military analysts, however, said they believed the President seemed overly alarmed when he talked of the unprecedented buildup.

The analysts said the main change they had seen recently in the disposition of Soviet military forces had been the tightening and testing of communication links between Moscow and military headquarters in Poland, East Germany and elsewhere in Eastern Europe.

In addition, they said the Soviet Union seems to have brought in new communication equipment to improve those links. But they said they had witnessed few communications among field visits themselves. Such communications, they said, would be indications that the units were preparing to move into action.

Other signs that apparently caused concern earlier in the week were the grounding of long-range Soviet air transports in the Soviet Union and Eastern Europe. Analysts say it now appeared they were grounded because of bad weather rather than in preparation for moving troops and weapons into action.

The next paragraph noted that Secretary of State Muskie said there was no evidence that the Soviet Union had decided to move into Poland and that other "analysts supported that by saying that there was no sign of tanks, the backbone of the Soviet army in that area, outside of the places in which they are usually found, and that no large units in either the Soviet Union or East Germany were moving toward Poland."

Almost predictably, an article on the following page (December 5:15) reported that Western sources said "that a Soviet armored division, normally stationed in East Germany was moving toward the East German–Polish border. . . . Further south another Soviet division was headed eastward from Berlin, the source said. The Soviet and East German Armies have announced maneuvers in the border area, but the sources did not comment on the purpose of the movements."

The appearance of the Gwertzman article illustrates that there does not exist an absolutely uniform, untextured hegemonic blanket that is draped over all news media activity and reports. Hegemonic ideology, as was noted earlier, successfully dominates cultural thinking, in part, because it permits, at least at its periphery, the appearance of alternative views. It is this appearance of variability that maintains the consistency of hegemonic domination with liberal ideals. We see the variability illustrated to some degree in the maybe-they-will-maybe-they-won't style of reporting that characterizes much of *Times* articles. The more dramatic and obvious cases such as the Gwertzman article appear less frequently, but do, nevertheless, appear. It is important to note that an article such as this one appeared in an "establishment" newspaper such as the *Times*. Regardless of the source, such counter-hegemonic perspectives indicate the possibility and fact of critical (regardless of how mild) vision within the hegemonic order. This suggests the further possibility of succeeding alternative hegemonies.

While it was not unusual for other articles to make note of the possibility that the Soviet Union might not launch an invasion, the Gwertzman article of December 5 was unique in that the dominant message communicated was not one of imminent military action. The next day (December 6:1), for example, although a front-page article headlined, "Soviet Bloc Nations Meet Unexpectedly in Crisis on Poland" carried the subhead "Diplomats Split on Meaning," and though it was reported that most Western officials said that the Polish government seemed to have won a breathing space from Moscow, it was reported that many thought the breathing space would be short. A senior diplomat was then quoted as saying that "this increases the pressure on Warsaw in a major way, and the Kremlin has left all its options open, including invasion." As usual, the dominant impression communicated was an ominous one. Evaluating a *Tass* report of the meeting, it was concluded,

Although the public language was conciliatory, especially in view of stern warnings to the Soviet Union from the West about the consequences of an intervention in Poland, the circumstances of the meeting seemed ominous to Western diplomats here as did a phrase in the *Tass* summary.

"The Polish People," the press agency said in its report, "can firmly count on the fraternal solidarity and support of the Warsaw Treaty nations."

The pattern of acknowledging alternative opinion and then rebutting it with "authoritative" comment continued through the rest of the article. After a European envoy was quoted as suggesting, "We must not discount the possibility that this meeting may have done more to take the heat out of the situation than to accentuate the crisis," the reader was informed,

Americans were skeptical of that viewpoint. "An invasion might be some time off," one said, "but Kania has been put into the dock and told that he has to do better than this." Like a number of others, he suggested that the Polish leader had probably been told to crack down and was given a time limit to deal with things himself before Moscow acted.

John Darnton's article on the front page of the "Week in Review" section of the next day's *Times* (December 7:1) made even less attempt to moderate the image of an aggressive Soviet Union. Headlined "Polish Winter, Prague Spring: Does Kremlin See a Difference?" the article avoided directly answering the question but, in a not at all subtle manner, provided a strong suggestion. A large map of Eastern Europe with the location and description of Soviet and Polish military forces dominated the page. Superimposed were two photographs. One photo was of Walesa speaking to workers in Gdansk. The second photo was captioned, "Czechoslovakia 1968: A Soviet Tank in a Prague Street."

The front-page headline the following day read, "Russians Are Ready for Possible Move on Poland, U.S. Says" (December 8:1). Subheads told of a White House warning but also that senior aides had reported that there was still no evidence of a Kremlin decision to intervene. Again, despite some acknowledgment of other interpretations, the conclusion was clear. While a few days earlier it had been possible to argue about whether the Soviets were on the verge of invasion, an official is quoted as declaring, "Now everyone agrees." Senior officials, it was reported, said "that the chance of a military move, probably conducted with Polish and other Warsaw Pact forces, was now more likely than not." The article was written by Gwertzman.

The next day it was reported that the Warsaw Pact nations had activated their reserves. Gwertzman (December 9:1) reported on the latest developments from the State Department while Danton (December 9:1) reported from Poland. After noting the reserve call-up, the second paragraph of Gwertzman's article informed the reader that "The State Department reported that it had no evidence of a decision to intervene in Poland, but there was reported agreement in the administration that some kind of intervention might be only days away." A senior official from the State Department was reported to have suggested that the invasion plan may have been drawn up at the summit in Moscow.

Darnton's article was primarily concerned with a piece in *Tass* that reported that counter-revolutionaries within Solidarity were attempting to destabilize Poland. It was reported that the *Tass* article might be used as a justification for invasion, and the buildup of forces at the Polish borders was again noted. Darnton then reported that information about these developments "is available to most Poles, who listened regularly to Western radio broadcasts. But many did not seem to regard an invasion as imminent and instead interpreted the buildup as an intense form of psychological pressure and as a sign to the leadership here that it must demonstrate its control." This characterization of the Polish attitude is particularly interesting. Why were Americans more suspicious of Soviet activities and intentions than were Poles who would seem to be at greater immediate risk? This issue does not receive extended attention within the article. In fact, the original observation is virtually denied later in the piece. On the jump page (p. 8) of the article, Darnton was to report that "In an attempt to calm the public, the editorial attacked what it called a 'hysterical campaign' in the Western news media about 'the alleged danger of military intervention from the outside.' "
The suggestion seems to be that first, the public needs to be calmed and second, that the criticism of Western media is a manipulative effort grounded in self-

interest. But what public requires calming? There is no indication that the Soviet audience is distressed, and Darnton himself had reported in the same article that the Poles do not fear an imminent invasion. By assigning a manipulative motive to the criticism, Darnton need not deal directly with the attack on the media.

Alarming reports about the Soviet invasion seemed to reach their crescendo during the next day or two. The *Times* military analyst, Drew Middleton, reported that Soviet forces were "fully prepared" to invade Poland, and that it was just the timing that remained uncertain (December 10:10). Articles originating from both the State Department (December 10:1) and Brussels (December 10:11) reported the efforts of Secretary of State Muskie to coordinate plans for a response to Soviet aggression and for the supply of radar planes to NATO "to counter the possibility of a surprise attack on Western Europe." The article from the State Department, by Gwertzman, reported that officials there "said the United States was not expecting the allies to agree formally to the steps contemplated by the United States at this time but rather to listen to the American presentation and indicate general backing." The reluctance of the allies to join the United States was not explained. Instead reference was made to the disappointment of the Carter administration with the Europeans' mild reaction to the Soviet invasion of Afghanistan. In one sentence, the impressions of the belligerence of the Soviet Union and the truculence of Western Europe were both reinforced without dealing directly with the issue of Western European resistance to the American interpretation of events and resulting policies.

The next day (December 11:1) it was Bernard Gwertzman who again provided an uncommon perspective on the issue of the impending Soviet invasion. After reporting that the Carter administration's constant warnings of an imminent Soviet invasion were a strategy to discourage the Soviets from invading, he observed that most senior officials within the administration felt, despite Washington's efforts, "that Moscow is embarked on such a course and is only waiting for the right moment to act." In the next paragraph, however, Gwertzman then reported that "there is a lingering doubt, particularly at the State Department, that the Russians will intervene." Gwertzman later in the article reinforces the point that assessment of Soviet intention is not uniform when he reported that the administration's policies "have caused some private exasperation in Western embassies, which are complaining about an excess zeal from the departing Administration." While the feeling among the embassies that the U.S. administration, with its zealous policies, had failed to take into account the Europeans' particular problems was acknowledged, the role of the media in the communication of that zeal to the American public was not considered or recognized. Again, though, Gwertzman's treatment of issues seems unique to the *Times* and particularly in comparison to the reporting found in the news magazines. While his reports certainly did not provide a systematic critique that would challenge the basic assumption of U.S. foreign policy, they did provide a more limited examination not found in other reports.

The Unlikely Soviet Invasion

Headlines and articles in the *Times* continued to sound alarm until just prior to a scheduled memorial service for workers killed in the 1970 demonstrations. In a report from Bucharest headlined, "Tension Over Poland Seems to Diminish in Rumania," a Rumanian official is quoted in the first paragraph as saying, "The danger exists and it would be a tragedy, and you could use all the adjectives you wanted to describe it. But I don't think the Russians wish to move in, and I think they are sincere" (December 14:20). Two days later an article with a Moscow dateline was headlined, "Soviet Obliquely Suggests Patient Stand on Poland" (December 16:11). In the first paragraph of this story it was reported that "The Soviet Union has suggested in a number of ways in the last three days that it is content, for the moment, to rely upon Poland's leaders to sort out that country's political and economic crises." About midway through the article the tone again became mixed, but included a sharper criticism than usual of U.S. handling of events. It was reported that Soviet officials

and an increasing number of Western European diplomats believe that Washington has overreacted to the Polish crisis, jumping to the conclusion that Soviet contingency maneuvers were the prelude to an invasion—"confusing capability with intent," as one European envoy said. Other analysts elsewhere note that this leaves open the question of what the Russians did intend when they began their maneuvers and whether the maneuvers could have been designed to put pressure on the Polish authorities to act—something they may be more inclined to do now than they were before the Soviet buildup.

In the next paragraph the reader was reminded that "Last year, Soviet official news organizations specifically denied that the Soviet armed forces were preparing to go into Afghanistan almost until they began moving in on Dec. 27." While the message is a mixed one, it is the dominant sense of relief that was being moderated rather than a sense of alarm.

Reports from elsewhere in Eastern Europe shared the more relaxed tone. One headline proclaimed that "Yugoslavia Is Alert But Calm on Poland" (December 16:13), and another that "Berliners Are Calm on Issue of Poland" (December 18:11). In the second article it was reported that a Soviet invasion was now seen by Western military authorities as unlikely, "at least until after the New Year," and that "Soviet forces surrounding Poland are still at maximum readiness and could be deep inside Poland within two hours. But there are signs of a general relaxation in the Polish crisis, American officials believe" (December 16:11).

An uncharacteristic headline of this time reported, "Hungarians Uneasy Over Polish Events" (December 21:4). The article attended more to concern that the labor unrest in Poland might spread elsewhere in Eastern Europe, though, than to concern about the possibility of a Soviet military action.

During this period the parties within Poland were reported to be developing a more cooperative relationship. Initially it was the church and government that were drawing closer. In a report (*NYT*, December 13:1) of a statement by Polish bishops warning of the dangers of action by political dissidents and extremists, it was noted that "During the strikes in August and September, the church, which commands the loyalty of 90 percent of Poland's 35 million people, issued appeals for calm and normalcy. But until now it has refrained from criticizing dissidents who in the past had found sanctuary for their activities in individual parishes." It was further noted that "There are other signs that the church and the party are drawing closer as Poland's crisis continues. A church–government commission to negotiate long-standing demands, including full legal status, has resumed meeting." It was then observed that the church had cooperated with the party before in times of crisis and that the present cooperation seemed to be motivated by "the concern that Poland's problems may soon bring in outside powers."

The memorial service proved to be the occasion for an "extraordinary display of unity" among the church, the party, and Solidarity. Darnton's report from Poland on the day of the service said that "the Roman Catholic Church, the Communist Party, and the new independent trade union called today for reconciliation, understanding and peace so that Poland can overcome its national crisis" (December 17:1). Darnton further observed that "The ceremony to commemorate the deaths, unthinkable only a year ago, was the high-water mark of the three-and-a-half-month workers' movement: a hopeful sign that the nation may draw together under the force of international tensions." The next day (December 18:13) an Associated Press article in the *Times* observed that "Mindful of the threat of Soviet intervention, union, church and party leaders have all appealed for calm and unity during this period of commemoration."

The Soviet Union, it seems, joined in the spirit of cooperation. Just prior to the memorial service John Darnton noted that "In the latest public suggestion that Moscow was willing to let Poland tend to its own troubles, at least for now, the Soviet press approvingly described speeches given this weekend by high-ranking Warsaw officials in which they said Poland's labor unrest posed no threat to the Soviet Union" (December 16:1).

Slight notice was given in the *Times* to any sign of dissension, though there was a United Press International report headlined, "Polish Dissident Criticizes Church" (December 21:3). Jacek Kuron, the "leader of Kor, the country's most outspoken dissident group," claimed that the church's criticism of dissidents served to spread rumors and increase social tension at a time when the government was already engaged in a campaign of slander against Kor. Such recognition of dissent—even while marginalizing that dissent—was unusual. More common were headlines such as "Polish Cardinal Appeals for Peace and Freedom" (December 25:3) on the occasion of the first live broadcast of Christmas mass in Poland since World War II, and "Brezhnev Assures Poland of Soviet's Trust" (December 27:3) on the occasion of Brezhnev's meeting with Poland's Foreign Minister Jozef Czyrek.

UNDERSTANDING THE INCONSISTENCIES

Clearly the reports and interpretations of events in Poland were greatly influenced not simply by activities within Polish society, but also by an American preoccupation with the Soviet Union. Few people would suggest that we could understand events in Poland without recognizing the Soviet presence—both actual and symbolic. But it is quite a different thing to permit our concern for the "Soviet threat" to define the situation for us.

Initially, particularly in the news magazines, the presentation of the issues, and of the sides, was clear. Solidarity, representing an anti-socialist, anti-Soviet force, were the "good guys." The socialist or Communist government of Poland and their Soviet puppeteers were the "bad guys." As the perception of the threat of Soviet military activity was seen to increase, the sides began to blur. Solidarity's insensitivities to the realities—as defined by the press—of the situation seemed to be providing the Soviet Union with an opportunity to expand its influence and military domination even further. The realistic and sensible Polish government seemed to be the only moderating factor in the developing situation.

Solidarity's noble cause had become less important than competitive big-power politics. In the *Times*, the Polish situation became most directly defined in terms of superpower issues. Characterization of the contending parties did not change so much in the *Times* as did attention to the issues. Poland and the struggle of its people to democratize and humanize its society ceased to receive the attention of the newspaper. Solidarity's cause was becoming invisible as it was being displaced by scenarios of Soviet expansionism.

Preexisting definitions of the world shaped news coverage of both the postal strike and Solidarity. The presentation of events was changed and strained to accommodate fundamental hegemonic definitions. Often similar developments were attributed inconsistent or conflicting meanings, depending upon their placement in either Poland or the United States.

The economic disruption in Poland caused by strikes organized by Solidarity, for example, were noted but it was not given attention of the same sort as the earlier American strike. In reporting on Poland, when the economic disruption and hardship were noted, they were presented either in the context of an already fragile Communist economy—such as was indicated by the headline, "Western *Times*" Economists Link Polish Trouble to an Inflexible System of Central Planning" (August 20:10)—or as an indication of the resolve of the Polish strikers.

In the postal strike the primary news frame focused attention on the actual or potential damage experienced by the business community. That community and "the economy" were seen as one. Business interests were presented as national interests. It was in the national interest that President Nixon called on the army to take over the postal system and break the strike. Presentation of the situation in the news accounts served to make such an act seem reasonable and prudent. Presentation of the Polish strikes would have made a similar government response, even if given the same official rationale, seem provocative and politically repressive.

Though the motivation and goals of the postal workers were initially endorsed on both the editorial and news pages of the *Times*, *Time*, and *Newsweek*, reporting in all three news organs was highly critical of the "desperate rejection of the law" that served to "endanger society." Law and order were of paramount importance. All other concerns, even if otherwise legitimate, must not violate the principles of law and the maintenance of order. Such claims of the importance of law and order by Polish authorities, however, were understood solely as a threat of the use of Soviet troops and increasingly extreme repression. This is so even though the words of Polish officials were often remarkably similar to those of U.S. officials. With but a change in the name of the nation, it could have been President Nixon, rather than Polish President Jablonski, who warned, "What is at stake is law and order in this country and something even bigger: Poland, the fate of the nation" (*NYT*, August 20:1).

The nonviolent nature of the Polish protests was presented prominently and served as evidence of the character of the workers and their commitment to peace and justice. Much attention was given to the nonviolent approach and the apparent religiosity of the workers. On the rare occasion that the issue of postal workers' nonviolent methods was noted at all, it was presented in a negative context, such as when it was warned that the activity of the postmen "underscores the helplessness of government in the face of organized, even if nonviolent, lawlessness" (*Time*, March 30:15).

It seems clear that it is the threat to the order of *American* society that defines concern for lawlessness. Laws in Poland are of little concern as they are simply means of Polish order. The commitment of Americans, and American journalists specifically, to a particular social order—that of the contemporary United States—defines their concern for law and order. That it is not order itself, but instead order of a particular sort, that is to be protected, even in the face of otherwise legitimate demands, is an indication of the cultural origins of the values that shape the presentation of news.

The value of and commitment to order is qualified. We are committed to an American order. Such an order, like any other, is characterized by particular social, political, and economic relationships, by particular relationships of power. When journalists defend the reasonable and prudent safeguard of law and order, they are promoting the legitimatization of particular social relations. It is their immersion in that network of relationships that has encouraged their absorption of a singular reality. They themselves become cultural expressions of that reality, with its particular social relationships, and consequently serve to reinforce those relationships. While the process, to some degree, characterizes all political participants, journalists, because of their unique position, serve a uniquely reinforcing function.

NOTE

1. A reader of the *New York Times* might wonder why the postal unions were characterized as being "politically powerful." If they had such power, why had the postal workers' frustration been ignored for so long? Even while acknowledging that the issues of contention had been long apparent, there was the suggestion that the final confrontation was the result of "power politics" and the refusal to recognize the needs of labor.

REFERENCES

Glasgow Media Group (1980) *More Bad News* (London: Routledge and Kegan Paul).
——— (1982) *Really Bad News* (London: Writers and Readers).
Knight, Graham (1982) "Strike Talk: A Case Study of News," *Canadian Journal of Communication* 8:61–79.

5
CONCLUSION

WHEN IT IS NOT SOVIETS WHO SHOUT

On August 17, 1986, two weeks short of the third anniversary of the shooting down of KAL 007, forces of the Sudanese People's Liberation Army shot down a twin-engine Sudan Airways passenger jet as it took off from Malakal on its way to Khartoum. All 63 people aboard the flight, all passengers and crew, were killed. There was no question about the identity of the flight or the intent of the rebels. The day before, the rebels had warned all aviators, including those flying civilian planes bringing food supplies to towns in the southern part of the country that had become isolated by war and flooding from the season's rains, that the aviators would fly at their own risk. Despite a critical food shortage and the potential of famine, the Sudanese People's Liberation Army was committed to putting an end to all flights into what they referred to as "War Zone No. 1."

This incident is interesting in the context of the present study for the telling comparisons it provides against the press treatment of KAL 007. There was no ambiguity in the Sudanese case. All parties involved agreed about what had happened, and the intentionality of the act was acknowledged. Not only was a civilian airliner carrying innocent passengers intentionally destroyed, but the people claiming responsibility asserted their intention to destroy any other flights even if their purpose was to provide food for people in need.

This act, it would seem from the perspective of Western sensibilities, would clearly qualify as an atrocity, a ruthless ambush and a wanton slaughter of innocent lives. This act, we would expect, would provoke the same horrified revulsion that characterized the response to the 007 incident in the American press. In fact, though, there was no such response. Reaction was not only subdued, but also quite limited. *Newsweek*, in the weeks following the shooting down of the Sudanese plane, did not have a single article about the event. *Time*, two weeks after the event, presented a one-page article of ten paragraphs noting the shooting and providing background on the conflict in Sudan (September 1, 1986:34). The report provided no hint of emotional involvement, concern, or crisis. Indeed, that the shooting occurred two weeks prior to the appearance of the article is an indication of the absence of urgency with which the incident was viewed.

The *New York Times* reported the shooting the day after it occurred. It was reported in headlines atop a front-page article, "Sudanese Airline with 60 on Board Downed by Missile" and "Southern Rebels Had Issued a Warning to Aviation—No Survivors Reported" (*NYT*, August 18:1). It might almost have seemed that the incident was the fault of the airline for not heeding the publicized warning. A second related article appeared the same day that explained how the "Sudanese Guerilla War Is Rooted in Deep Ethnic Divisions" (*NYT*, August 18:4).

The following day a page 8 headline read, "Red Cross Suspends Sudan Flights After Downing of Plane by Rebels" (*NYT*, August 19:8). The next day the only mention of the incident was in the "Around the World" column, where a four-paragraph piece was headlined, "U.N. Reveals Decision to Halt Food to Sudan" (*NYT*, August 20:7). The day after that note an article carried the headline, "Aid Teams Wary About the Sudan," with the subhead of "Relief Officials Say Rebel War Could Lead to a Famine as Bad as Ethiopia's in' '85" (*NYT*, September 21:3). The following day there was no news from Sudan.

The differences in the press treatment of the two cases of civilian airliners being destroyed is extraordinary. It might be suggested that the differences can be explained by the fact that Americans were immediately involved—both as victims and traffic controllers—in one case but not in the other. While there might seem to be some sense to this suggestion at first glance, it certainly does not explain the extremes—in extended coverage (both in terms of space and time) and in the emotional intensity of the coverage—that characterize the treatment of the KAL incident. The difference can instead be best explained, particularly in light of this study, by recognizing how the participation of the Soviet Union in the KAL incident served to provide the definition and provoke the emotional intensity of the coverage. It was not the act of murdering innocent civilians that provoked press response in the KAL incident as much as it was the actor who committed the murder. The frame used to present the shooting of KAL 007 was of the evil Soviet Union that committed a horrific act. The act was interpreted as horrific, apparently, because it was an act of the Soviets. While the facts surrounding the act were acknowledged to be ambiguous, the definition of the act was not. On the other hand, when the civilian flight in Sudan was shot down the facts were clear and unambiguous. But the press's definition of the act was not as categorical.

An understanding of the press, or more generally, the news media, as merely an information conduit, as "simply noisy channels which connect one end of the information exchange with another" (Hall 1975:17) is unable to provide an explanation of the differences in presentation of the shootings or the other patterns of presentation examined here. Information is not simply collected and transferred to the reader, listener, or viewer. While objective journalism, like an objective, scientific sociology that studies it, is supposed to be realized in accordance with professionally defined activity consistent with recognized, appropriate methods (Tuchman 1980:11), neither the journalist nor the social scientist is simply a facilitator or vehicle through which unadulterated facts pass. The collection, dissemination, and reception of news is, like the sociological enterprise, a social process. The necessary social nature of the process makes the "fact transferral" characterization of the press unavoidably problematic.

Information is not simply collected. Rather, selected information is organized by journalists whose task it is to create a flowing narrative from "facts" fished from the flow of history. Both the identification of individual entities or "fact units" and their subsequent narrative organization assumes a knowledge of the world that is necessarily social in origin. There is no Archimedean point on which the journalist, or any of us, can locate ourselves apart from some social context, some social reality. The journalist sees with the lens provided by his/her culture and writes to an audience that is expected to be viewing the world in a similar manner.

ON FACTS THAT SPEAK FOR THEMSELVES

It has been suggested (Epstein 1981) that there are facts that are beyond interpretation or contention. These facts are understood to "speak for themselves." Examples of the reporting of such facts include reports of closing stock prices, racetrack results, weather, or Reuters news service operation of food warehouse temperatures for food shippers. According to Epstein:

In this form of reporting, there is no analysis or journalistic bias. The "targets" are selected by the news organization on the calculus of profitability; the space is allocated to the scores for which audiences will presumably pay the most money—or which will attract the greatest number of readers. (1981:121)

The "calculus of profitability" though is itself an artifact of a particular kind of social order. That decision-making orientation, along with that which is reported, is produced by and reproduces that order. While the reporting of facts of the sort identified by Epstein may not include analysis, they do, nevertheless, illustrate a journalistic bias. By reporting the worth of specific stocks and the vagaries of the market as a whole on a daily basis, the stock market is presented as, understood to be, and maintained as a primary indication of national economic health. (This despite the fact that 80 percent of all stock is owned by less than

2 percent of the population [Eitzen 1986:34].) Stock trading rather than unemployment rates (which are reported monthly) or poverty rates (which are reported yearly) or some other such measures of the costs of the economic organization of society are promoted as a standard of economic health. With extremes of wealth and poverty becoming increasingly exaggerated (Ehrenreich 1986:44), this type of reporting becomes particularly insidious, as the stock market is exceptionally profitable for its investors at the same time the poor are becoming increasingly numerous. Interestingly, such reporting also communicates that a prized manner in which to accumulate wealth is through fortuitous, even if informed, investment. Investment, rather than "hard work," is the way to riches. But investment is a privilege available only to those with expendable wealth. Stock reports then serve to legitimate the practice—and the right—of monied people to accumulate or "earn" more money without working for it.

If even the reporting of stock prices, an exemplar of objective facts, illustrates a commitment to and the promotion of a particular kind of social organization, it would seem that the model of objectivity provided below, a model that eschews subjectivity, partisanship, and partiality, is an impossibility that denies the unavoidable social nature of the activities of journalists.

The canon of objectivity requires that news should offer as complete a capture of events in the world as possible, and that the presentation of those accounts should not be shaped by the personal values or commitments of the journalists involved. The ideal of objectivity then, rests on the claim that news is accurate, comprehensive and neutral, and consists of independently verifiable facts that are clearly separated from expression of opinions or values. (Murdock 1980:460)

This formulation of objectivity and the avoidance of bias rests on two related assumptions. The first is that the failure to be objective and to avoid bias is the failure of individuals. The second assumption is that an unmediated contact can be made with the facts of the world. Both assumptions are avoidably problematic.

The assumption that the failure to achieve objectivity is personal in origin, that it is the bias "of the reporter [we] see on television or whose by-line is at the top of the article . . . reduces the issue to one of personal fairness (or ignorance), and the remedy most often suggested is to replace or educate the newsman." For Epstein, "This focus on personal bias tends to distract attention from the more important issue of organizational bias" (Epstein 1981:125). I would suggest that a focus limited to either individual journalists or individual organizations, while informative, blinds us to the most significant values and biases that shape journalistic work, those that originate in our hegemonic social/political culture. The education of journalists and the modification or moderation of organizational demands are shaped within a specific and particular culture. Individual and organizational possibilities, and professional goals—such as the achievement (and even the definition) of objective journalistic production—are shaped by the social context within which they exist.

That we can have unmediated, direct contact with social reality is the second of the problematic assumptions. That a journalist can capture reality and then present it, and that others can evaluate the accuracy of that presentation assumes a reality with which we can achieve an experience of immediacy free from the imposition of any mediation. This conception of the possibilities of the relationship between the individual and the objective world is shared by most social scientists as well as journalists. Indeed, as McQuail (1985) points out, many of the social scientific studies most critical of journalism and the biases journalists represent assume knowledge of a reality that has been distorted by news journalists.

It should be apparent though that different cultures "see" the world differently. Whether we are comparing ourselves who see "snow" with Laplanders who see dozens of different types of snow, or ourselves who see Solidarity as an anti-socialist movement with the Poles of Solidarity who see the movement as one combating Soviet imperialism, the lens of societal experience is seen to color the variety of individual experiences. It would be misleading to understand the different "seeings" or the different "knowledges" simply as an intriguing artifact of geographical position on the globe, as another indication of the wonders of the different ways in which human groups have organized their lives. The world in which we come to have knowledge about the world, is of a particular sort, a particular order. Though the order is always evolving (or better, changing) and never absolutely secure, it does represent a particular constellation of social relations or a particular integration of the institutions of society. The manner of integration, of organization, indicates and serves to reproduce particular priorities, values, and interests. News that informs us of the world, from the perspective of any particular world, will reflect those priorities, values, and interests. News, then, is not simply a "constructed reality" (see Molotch and Lester 1974), but instead a reality constructed within a particular social/political/economic ecology.

AMERICAN HEGEMONIC REALITY

The presentation of the world examined in the present work seems shaped more by images and understandings originating in an American social/political/economic ecology than by the events themselves. This American, capitalist filter has colored the journalism. It colored the shooting of a civilian airliner that occurred under ambiguous circumstances in categorial tones. Earlier the filter painted strikes within our own nation as disturbances and threats to effective and efficient economic function (economic efficacy, defined in terms of administrative concerns, is seen as a measure of national excellence), and strikes outside our borders in colors dependent upon how those strikes reflected upon the economic and social systems of that nation and consequently upon capitalist economies. The filter suggests that a violation of law, particularly law that defines economic relationships, be sharply rebuked, unless such violation occurs in a nation characterized by economic relationships that we understand to conflict with our own. Collective action and mass movements are seen, through the filter, not in terms defined by the participants themselves, but instead in terms of the significance of the movement, both symbolic and actual, to the valued American order and the perceptions supporting that order.

Two primary elements of U.S. hegemonic ideology can be understood to be closely related. While hegemonic ideology is not fully integrated and consistent, neither is it the chance coalescence of isolated perspectives. The anti-Soviet, anti-socialist, and pro-business aspects of the hegemonic filter are closely related. The Soviet Union, or more fundamentally, socialism, represents an order that violates the basic assumptions of U.S. economic arrangements. We need not assume that socialist forces aim at world military domination to understand those forces as a potential threat to capitalism. The assumptions of socialism conflict with those of societies with capitalist economies. A full consideration of the assumptions of socialism would permit the possibility of a critique of capitalism and its assumptions. It is when alternative information and interpretations or world views are accessible that a critique has the potential to replace skepticism and even to undermine approval. (See Murdock [1980] for a discussion of the difference between skepticism and critique.) Efforts to discredit the socialist order, or more immediately the symbols of that order, limit the availability of alternative models of reality and inhibit the possibility of a comprehensive critique of the capitalist order: "The stability of our societies may depend, not so much upon consensus concerning particular values or norms, but upon a lack of consensus at the very point where oppositional attitudes could be translated into political action" (Thompson 1984:5). The priority of business concerns in the coverage of the postal strike and the anti-Soviet framing of the activities in Poland and of the KAL 007 incident then are not unrelated. Pro-business and anti-Soviet or anti-socialist perspectives rest on opposing sides of the same coin.

The priority of business interests, and the identification of those interests as the "national interest," shaped coverage of the postal strike. What was the threat presented by the "lawless" postal union? The strike was not, it would seem, causing any physical or mortal harm to anyone. It was not destroying any physical property. The strike was a violation of labor law. Strikers were refusing to comply with the established, regulated procedures of labor–management relations. Further, it was defying the government, which is, in the last resort, responsible for the enforcement of those procedural relations.

It is obviously not the simple violation of the law that is responsible for the adoption of a particular frame used to report the strike. Solidarity also engaged in unlawful activity, but that was the violation of Polish law. White collar and corporate crime occurs all the time, but such lawlessness does not get the headlines of the postal strike. The strike of postal workers represented something of particular importance other than simply a violation of law. It represented the violation of something more basic than the law—the violation of basic social, that is, property relationships. The violation of regulated procedures of labor–

management relations represents the potential violation or rejection of the social relations on which the system is based. The defiance of the government—in this case by federal workers—represents a rejection of the legal legitimacy that supports those relations. Rejection of such law in the United States is viewed contemptuously. Rejection of such law in Poland, viewed through American political culture, is cause for celebration, as it represents the rejection of socialist social relations. The order maintained by rule of law is order of a particular sort with particular interests protected (Gans 1979:57). As Americans, we are concerned about order of the type that maintains social relations only of a specific sort.

The protection of domestic order is accomplished by the media's representation of international as well as domestic news. International relations for Americans, are, for the most part, understood as a conflict between East and West, or more specifically, between the Soviet Union and the United States. Most events outside our borders, and many inside are interpreted in the context of this omnipresent conflict. The destruction of a Korean airliner becomes a statement of an adversary's (the Soviet Union's) character. Poland understood simply as a pawn of the Soviet bear is seen as an expression of the evils of socialism. (There is little distinction in meaning between socialism and the Soviet Union in this view.) Consequently, a social movement within Poland, which is anti-Soviet, is to be supported. If it is anti-Soviet, it must also be anti-socialist. That is, primarily, how Solidarity was represented—as an anti-Soviet, anti-socialist movement. This manner of presentation is consistent with Gans's (1979) observation that news stories about Communist bloc nations frequently concern internal problems and government failures. Most description particularly early in the coverage of Solidarity fit into this package, or frame. Certainly, a "revolt" against the political/ economic system represents both a problem for the government and a failure. Such presentation, however, obscures, or more accurately, denies the fact that while Solidarity was, in fundamental ways, anti-Soviet, it was not anti-socialist. If attention were paid to the demands of Solidarity it would have been recognized that its aims were, in large part, to democratize Polish socialism and to ensure actual worker independence and responsibility in place of state bureaucratic domination of the workplace. Indeed, in an article likening a propaganda attack of the Polish government on Kor—which served as an advisory group to Solidarity and was described in a United Press International release as "the country's most outspoken dissident group" (*NYT*, December 21:3)—to McCarthyism, trying to illustrate the organization's self-circumscribed goals, Darnton suggested:

No one in the group talks of doing away with socialism or prying Poland loose from the Warsaw Pact alliance. They accept the realities of the country's geographic position and work instead for reform of socialism and for human rights. Their attacks on socialism in Poland concentrated on what they construe as its repression and its deformations—party privileges, the new elite and mismanagement. (*NYT*, November 16:4;1)

The filter of American hegemonic ideology prevented the recognition that Polish nationalism aims to serve Polish, not American, anti-Soviet interests.

It was the American anti-socialist, anti-Soviet preoccupation that was the basis of the frame used to report the Korean airliner incident. It was also the basis of the original frame used to present Solidarity—a disciplined, justified mass movement of reasonable, committed people—and the subsequent frame—a provocative, undisciplined, unreasonable movement courting national suicide. As illustrated, the initial presentation of strikers and their leadership was entirely favorable. By December, however, a dramatic change was taking place. In the news magazines the personal motivation of Solidarity leadership was under question, the movement itself was seen to be getting out of control, to be acting irresponsibly, and the Polish government was beginning to be pictured as the reasonable, moderating force. In the *Times*, the anti-socialist/anti-Soviet preoccupation was expressed in the original frame followed by the explicit use of the Soviet-invasion frame. If we understand the origins of the KAL presentation in the news and the initial interpretation of the Solidarity movement, we can understand the subsequent characterization of Solidarity. At the same time that the change of frames was developing in the coverage of events in Poland, a corresponding change was occurring in the assessment of an imminent Soviet invasion that was understood to provide an opportunity for further Soviet military involvement in Europe. Since it was American understanding of and concern about socialism and the Soviet Union that was the ground in which the original frame developed, it should not be surprising that it was the same understanding and concern that provoked the subsequent frame. The bear, it seemed, might be strengthened rather than tweaked. A re-understanding of events was therefore required. The frame within which events in Poland were pictured became modified to meet the requirements of the perceived changes of the situation.

It might be suggested that the change in frames reflected not the development of an alternative understanding among journalists, but instead the change in the U.S. government's definition of the situation. The press, in this view, was simply reporting the changes in government perception. It was reporting the activities and statements of the government and its representatives, not its own perceptions and analysis. The press, in this view, is seen as a marionette that is manipulated by the government, dutifully relaying the reality provided by government spokespeople (official and unofficial) and government press releases. Such a suggestion, however, ignores a long history of discussion about the government–press relationship (for example, Hachlen 1963; Minor 1970; Bagdakian 1974; Gormley 1975; Connell 1979; Gans 1979; Steinberg 1980; Blumler and Gurevitch 1981; Grossman and Kumar 1981). The press need not be at the end of the government's strings to come to provide the public with the government's view of the world. The fundamentals of the government position will be accepted because journalists share the logic of the position (Connell 1979). Journalists share the assumptions and understandings that represent the culture's hegemonic world view. Even when questions are addressed to the government's declarations, they usually reflect differences over strategy or approach to shared concerns rather than violations of basic, hegemonic assumptions.

The dependence of the press on government statements and government sources, both official and unofficial, represents a particular attitude toward the U.S. government—its credibility and its motivation, and that of alternative sources. It is not all governments that speak with authority and truth; it is the U.S. government that does so. This becomes most apparent when statements from Moscow are summarily dismissed as "half-truths and outright lies" and when statements of the Polish government are viewed in the American press with suspicion. Walesa, Kuron, and other labor and dissident figures were relied upon for credible assessments of events. The word of labor leaders, at least in the first months of Solidarity, was presented as more plausible and trustworthy than that of government. Statements by the government were examined for the hidden or suggested meaning and intentions they represented. Statements by representatives of Solidarity went unchallenged. For the most part, Solidarity had credibility similar to the sort possessed by the U.S. government. This is particularly telling, given the press treatment of labor common in Western industrialized nations (Beharrell and Philo 1977; Glasgow Media Group 1976, 1980, 1982; Knight 1982; Morley 1976). In East bloc nations it is the government sources who were suspect, as the government itself is understood to be illegitimate. The suspicion, of course, reinforces the sense of illegitimacy.

That government sources are not routinely and automatically seen to be credible is most apparent when the sources are Soviet. Statements by representatives of the Soviet government or reports appearing in the government press were constantly and soberly examined for any messages and intentions that might be discerned from the subtext. Intention in these cases was routinely a matter for discovery. Reliance on U.S. government sources for dependable, credible information, then, indicates a particular attitude toward the U.S. government. Intention and motivation, in the case of such sources, are not problematic and remain, on the whole, unquestioned.

Again, reliance on sources within the U.S. government, and Western European governments when appropriate, is not due simply to their accessibility or habitual and institutionalized patterns of government–press communication. Such reliance instead rests more fundamentally on assumptions of trust that require little or no accountability. Press and government both accept unquestioningly the same givens. They share the same fundamental political assumptions. They share a common hegemonic ideology or world view. This shared understanding is then the basis for the trust and reliance. This trust and reliance is, of course, mutual. The President, for example, would not expose himself to news conferences— even if only on an irregular basis—if the press could not be relied upon and trusted to have accepted and be committed to maintaining an only moderately "adversarial" relationship. (See Chapter 2, Note 1, for an example of what happens when the commonly accepted bounds of appropriateness are violated.) Again, a preexisting orientation or world view shapes the coverage and presentation of news.

The changes in frames used to present events in Poland, and the occasional skepticism—even if only moderate—directed toward statements of U.S. asministrations illustrate a central feature of hegemony. Important aspects of hegemony are seen to be fluid or, at least, flexible. Indeed, this is an aspect of hegemony that permits it to be maintained. Fundamental elements of the world view must remain immutable, but the supportive structure can be adjusted to meet the requirements of change and of history. These changes appear quite natural as they are consistent with the most basic elements of our understanding of our social world, even if they are inconsistent with some supporting elements within the same world view. The contradictions within hegemonic ideology and the presence of voices of skepticism within hegemonically dominated institutions provide opportunity for counter-hegemonic realities.

The degree to which the American political culture and, consequently, its press is anti-socialist and, in turn, anti-Soviet, does not reflect a requirement necessary to maintain democratic capitalism. Clearly, while sharing many similarities with the press of the United States, the Canadian press examined here was more textured and varied. Western European politics certainly reflects a wider range of political discussion than is found in the United States. Variety in the press, either within individual newspapers and magazines or in the range of available newspapers and magazines, reflects the considered political possibilities. The United States appears unique, if not in its common identification of clearly enunciated political values and principles, then in its aversion to all that is considered, within the confines of our political culture, to be immoderate. Such a culture leaves Americans not with a press filled with debate on issues, both fundamental and pragmatic (if such a distinction can be made), but instead with a "mainstream" press, reflecting significant variations not in political commitment but instead in "quality," and an "alternative" press of limited availability, more limited readership, and most limited impact. (See Landry, Morley, and Southwood [1984] on the difficulties faced by the alternative press.) The hegemonic political culture that defined the possibilities of the press is, at the same time, championed by that press.

The press, while it reproduces the hegemony within which it exists, contains also the possibilities of counter-hegemonies. The social system reproduced by and shaping the press is itself characterized by contradiction and conflict. As these conflicts and contradictions find their way into the news—even if indirectly—they find an articulation that can attract attention to them and promote awareness and understanding of them. In the provision of negative models that develop from the skepticism resulting from inconsistencies and contradictions experienced, and read, the ground is provided for positive models that make possible, though not inevitable, the critique from which to build the foundation of counter-hegemonies.

CONCLUSION

Despite itself then, the press can provide the opportunity for creation rather than simply re-creation. Ironically, it is because the social order holds within itself the possibility of change, that the press can become a counter-hegemonic tool. It is in this manner too, that the press becomes a tool of democracy. While in times of normalcy the press certainly does not promote the conditions suggested in the quote below to be required by democracy, neither does it, as some would suggest, make it impossible to achieve.

[I]f there is to be democracy, citizens when they make political choices, must have intelligible, relevant and genuinely different alternatives to choose between, and the men who put alternatives to them must have sufficient motives for putting alternatives of this kind. (John Plamenatz, quoted in Blumler 1983:180)

Until the conditions described by Plamenatz are realized, it is the responsibility of those interested in the news media and committed to democracy to maximize the press's (latent) democratic potential. The study of the press, the examination of journalism and journalistic practice needs to be redirected. While he is clearly not without reservation about such an effort, Gans (1983:183) begins to identify the concerns of such study.

[N]ews media researchers with an interest in policy must begin to propose and discuss other means with which to evaluate news. This is a difficult venture, because ultimately such evaluations are based on the purposes one assigns to the news media and on what one considers to be the essential elements of democracy.

A reorientation of the study of the press, away from the traditionally defined issues of objectivity, bias, and the like, and instead toward evaluation according to the standard of democracy (a reorientation that would, as Gans suggests, necessitate a discussion of what we, as Americans, mean by democracy—an invaluable and, no doubt, enlightening discussion) would force the recognition of the press as something other than an asocial, ahistorical communication medium.

Such study would both diminish and strengthen the force of the press. The ability of the media to secure consent is, in large part, due to its accepted claims of freedom and independence. An examination of the press in the broad social context within which it functions would identify its legal freedoms and journalistic independence within cultural constraints and socially constructed limitations. Press freedom and independence, when recognized to be not absolute but instead quite relative and restricted, might cease to be a source of its, and the social order's, legitimacy. As the ability or right of the press to identify and define issues is diminished, the press as a forum for the discussion of issues could be maximized. The force and influence could then become maximized as a democratic instrument.

This scenario, of course, has not yet acknowledged the obvious, immediate, and pragmatic difficulties of realizing a press seen as a sort of minutes of a town (nation) meeting. As the hegemonic ideology reflected in and by the news media represents, re-presents, and re-creates the relations of power that characterize the social order, a redefinition of the standards and purpose of the press will not be met without resistance—systemic, institutional and individual. The press shows us though—if we did not know it already—that the forces of domination are wrought with contradictions and conflicts that cannot be concealed indefinitely. These conflicts and contradictions themselves become the fertile ground in which intelligible, relevant, and genuinely different alternatives can take root.

It is hoped that the present work will contribute to the democratization of American society by its identification of inconsistencies and conflicts within our political culture and more specifically within an instrument of that culture—the news media. If we take the study of the press beyond the parochial concerns of individual journalists, particular organizations, and the journalistic profession and instead recognize the press's location in the totality of social life, including (but not limited to) the political culture of a society—its dominant values, ideas, concerns, its hegemonic ideology—we can recognize how the press serves to inhibit imagination and limit the possibilities of social relationships. Not until there are genuine alternatives, recognized as real, realizable choice possibilities can democratic ideals be realized. If democracy is intended to provide the opportunity for self-determination, it requires that the spectrum of possible realities be limited only during the process of self-determining and not by the social arrangements that are themselves to be evaluated. Lived experience and the institutions that secure that experience must be examined and evaluated. Such examination and evaluation must be part of both the democratic and sociological agendas.

REFERENCES

Bagdakian, Ben H. (1974) "Congress and the Media: Partners in Propaganda," *Columbia Journalism Review* 12:3–10.

Beharrell, P., and G. Philo (1977) *Trade Unions and the Media* (London: Macmillan).

Blumler, Jay G. (1983) "Communication and Democracy: The Crisis Beyond and the Ferment Within," *Journal of Communication* 33:166–73.

Blumler, Jay G., and Michael Gurevitch (1981) "Politicians and the Press: An Essay on Role Relationships," in *Handbook of Political Communication*, edited by Dan D. Nimmo and Keith R. Sanders (Beverly Hills, CA: Sage), pp. 467–93.

Connell, Ian (1979) "Television, News and the Social Contract," *Screen* 20:87–107.

Ehrenreich, Barbara (1986) "Is the Middle Class Doomed?" *New York Times Magazine*, September 7, 1986:44–64.

Eitzen, D. Stanley (1986) *Social Problems*, 3rd edn (Boston, MA: Allyn and Bacon).

Epstein, Edward Jay (1981) "The Selection of Reality," in *What's News: The Media in American Society*, edited by Elie Abel (San Francisco, CA: Institute for Contemporary Studies), pp. 119–32.

Gans, Herbert J. (1979) *Deciding What's News* (New York: Random House).

―――― (1983) "News Media, News Policy, and Democracy: Research for the Future," *Journal of Communication* 33:174–84.
Glasgow Media Group (1976) *Bad News* (London: Routledge and Kegan Paul).
―――― (1980) *More Bad News* (London: Routledge and Kegan Paul).
―――― (1982) *Really Bad News* (London: Writers and Readers).
Gormley, William Thomas Jr. (1975) "Newspaper Agendas and Political Elites," *Journalism Quarterly* 52:304–8.
Grossman, M., and M. Kumar (1981) *Portraying the President: The White House and the News Media* (Baltimore, MD: Johns Hopkins University).
Hachlen, William A. (1963) "The Press as Reporter and Critic of Government," *Journalism Quarterly* 40:12–18.
Hall, Stuart (1975) "Introduction," in *Paper Voices: The Popular Press and Social Change, 1935–1965*, edited by A.C.H. Smith (London: Chatto and Windus), pp. 11–24.
Knight, Graham (1982) "Strike Talk: A Case Study of News," *Canadian Journal of Communication* 8:61–79.
Landry, Charles, David Morley, and Russell Southwood (1984) "The Alternative Press: The Development of Underdevelopment," *Media, Culture and Society* 6:95–102.
McQuail, Denis (1985) "Sociology of Mass Communication." *Annual Review of Sociology* 11:93–111.
Minor, Dale (1970) *The Information War: How Government and the Press Manipulate, Censor and Distort the News* (New York: Hawthorn).
Molotch, Harvey, and Marilyn Lester (1974) "News As Purposeful Behavior: On the Strategic Use of Routine Events, Accidents and Scandals," *American Sociological Review* 39:101–12.
Morley, David (1976) "Industrial Conflict and the Mass Media," *Sociological Review* 24:245–68.
Murdock, Graham (1980) "Misrepresenting Media Sociology: A Reply to Anderson and Sharrock," *Sociology* 14:457–68.
Steinberg, Charles S. (1980) *The Information Establishment: Our Government and the Media* (New York: Hastings House).
Thompson, John B. (1984) *Studies in the Theory of Ideology* (Berkeley, CA: University of California).
Tuchman, Gaye (1980) "The Facts of the Moment: The Study of News," *Symbolic Interaction* 3:9–20.

APPENDIX A: PRIMARY FOCUS OF *NEW YORK TIMES* ARTICLES ABOUT POLAND AND SOLIDARITY (August 8, 1980–December 31, 1980)

Week	Internal Affairs S*	Internal Affairs M*	Internal Affairs L*	U.S.S.R. S	U.S.S.R. M	U.S.S.R. L	Other S	Other M	Other L
Aug. 8–14	3	—	—	—	—	—	—	1	—
Aug. 15–21	1	9	2	2	2	1	4	1	—
Aug. 22–28	—	3	10	3	5	2	5	5	1
Aug. 29–Sept. 4	2	9	7	2	3	—	6	7	—
Sept. 5–11	3	6	4	2	1	—	3	5	—
Sept. 12–18	1	7	1	—	2	—	1	1	—
Sept. 19–25	1	4	—	2	2	—	2	—	—
Sept. 26–Oct. 2	3	4	—	1	1	—	1	—	—
Oct. 3–9	1	2	—	—	—	—	—	—	—
Oct. 17–23	1	2	—	1	2	—	—	—	—
Oct. 24–30	—	4	1	—	3	—	—	—	—
Oct. 31–Nov. 6	—	3	—	—	1	—	1	—	—
Nov. 7–13	2	7	—	2	—	—	1	—	1
Nov. 14–20	2	8	—	2	1	—	—	1	—
Nov. 21–27	2	8	—	1	2	—	—	1	—
Nov. 28–Dec. 4	1	3	—	4	7	—	—	1	—
Dec. 5–11	1	4	—	5	16	2	1	1	—
Dec. 12–18	—	6	—	8	13	1	1	3	—
Dec. 19–25	6	2	—	—	6	—	3	—	—
Dec. 26–31	1	2	—	1	2	1	—	—	—

* S, M, L—Article length as noted in *Times* Index. (L) indicates a long story over 3 columns, (M) indicates a medium-length story between 1 and 3 columns, and (S) indicates a short item of less than 1 column.

SUMMARY OF APPENDIX A

	Internal Affairs	U.S.S.R.	Other
Aug. 8–28	28	20	17
Aug. 29–Sept. 25	45	14	26
Sept. 26–Oct. 30	20	9	1
Oct. 31–Nov. 27	32	9	5
Nov. 28–Dec. 31	26	66	10

APPENDIX B: A NOTE ON METHODS

THE EVENTS EXAMINED

At first glance it might seem that there is little relationship among matters such as the Soviet shooting of KAL 007, a strike of U.S. postal workers, and the Solidarity movement in Poland. Examination of the press's treatment of these matters, however, permits the identification of patterns that enable us to understand how events and issues come to be defined for presentation in the news.

Presentation of the KAL incident provided the most apparent and obvious example of how the American press uses preexisting definitions of the world—and specifically of the United States, the Soviet Union, and their relationship—to understand or explain events. Rather than providing a narrative of an unfolding of events or capturing the dynamism of historical processes, world events were seen instead shaped to fit the preexisting definitions and categories.

The comparison of Canadian press with that of the United States was intended to determine the necessity of the American presentation (that is, was it simply a "true," "objective" presentation that resulted from the freedom and independence that characterize the press in the United States—a highly unlikely possibility given the inconsistencies and contradictions noted in the presentations) and whether such a manner of presentation might be understood to be necessary to the preservation of Western, liberal, democratic interests (that is, a reformulation of the journalism-as-patriotism issue).

Consideration of the presentation of the KAL 007 incident in *Granma* was included to identify some of the differences, and similarities, found between a free press and a state-controlled press. While the force of political culture serves some of the same ends as the force of the state, the manner in which it works is significantly different and the texture—and potential—of the resulting product is quite different.

Having noted the virulent anti-Soviet presentation that characterized the coverage of

KAL 007 in the American press, examination of the presentation of the postal strike and Solidarity was intended to provide an understanding of the significance of that indicated attitude. A consideration of the treatment of Solidarity in light of treatment of a strike by federal workers in the United States was intended to identify more clearly the nature of the concerns that characterized coverage of Solidarity. A comparison of alternative frames used to present similar aspects of these two events (that were obviously also significantly dissimilar in fundamental ways) was intended to help us understand the origin of the frames used and thereby more fully understand the manner in which hegemonic world views shape news accounts.

The comparison of domestic and foreign strikes also permitted the identification of issues or values that are common in both. The combination of comparisons of events and press permitted the identification of the most fundamental value of the preservation of a domestic capitalist order as the common source of frames used in the news accounts examined. Whether it is a criticism of socialist economic and political organization, critical portrayal of a "communist" adversary, or a direct defense of capitalist social relations, the press presentation serves to preserve capitalist order by criticizing the assumptions of alternatives, providing the negative examples of the horrific results of societies understood to be structured by socialist design, and by directly promoting an identification of capitalism as nationalism.

The Press Examined

The reputation of the *New York Times* as a standard of journalistic excellence and as a newspaper of record that is of great influence in providing definition for events of our world made it an obvious selection to be included in this study. *Time* and *Newsweek* were included as they represent the newsweeklies with the greatest circulation and are therefore influential in that respect. Comparisons between the daily and the weeklies provided examples of differences in style and content, but, more strikingly, indicated a sharing of the basic premises that define the culture's hegemonic world view.

The *Globe and Mail* and *Maclean's* represent the Canadian counterparts to the American press studied and were selected for that reason. Canadian journalism was selected as a source of comparison to American journalism for the geographical and cultural proximity of Canada and the U.S. Differences found in the presses of these nations could be more informative than those found in a comparison of the American press with that of Western or Eastern Europe or another area of the world with which the United States did not have as much in common. Consideration of accounts from other nations would, no doubt, have added some to our understanding of the subtleties of the process and content of hegemony. Consideration of accounts in the "alternative" press in the United States would similarly have provided additional insight, as would have the consideration of television news, but such efforts were beyond the intent of this undertaking and will have to wait for later projects.

Granma is included in this study, as suggested earlier, because it provided some comparison between free and state-controlled presses. Though Cuba was not directly involved in the KAL incident, it could be expected to provide an alternative perspective to that provided in the American and Canadian presses. The degree to which it relied on the Soviet news service was unanticipated but provided insight into both the direct connections between the press of the two nations and into the Soviets' own presentation of news.

Articles about 007 in the American press from the time of the incident on August 31, 1983 through the end of the year and then on or about the first and second anniversaries of the event were examined. The *Globe and Mail* was examined for the two weeks after the incident until it was no longer front-page news. *Maclean's* was examined until it included no stories of the incident. *Granma* was examined from the first issue after the shooting until the first week news of the incident failed to appear in the newspaper (October 9). Coverage of the postal strike that appeared in the *Times* between March 19, 1970 and April 3, 1970 and in *Time* and *Newsweek* from March 23, 1970 to April 6, 1970 was examined. News of Solidarity in the *Times* and the newsweeklies from August 1980 to the end of the year was examined.

Literary/Linguistic Analysis

It has been suggested (Garnham 1983:317) that British media studies originated in the tradition of a "methodology based upon detailed textual analysis and a concern with sociocultural values and meanings that was actually hostile to positivist empirical sociology, seeing that description and its methods as themselves a cultural symptom of the alienating effects of capitalist development." A method of content analysis based in the assumptions of positivism and its definition of scientific research, then, prevented an understanding of the media and obscured that which was of concern and interest. On this side of the Atlantic, it has been observed that the "quantitative techniques pioneered by Lazarsfeld, his associates and students, were not suited to a critical exploration of the role of the media in American life" (Tuchman 1980:9), and a call has been made for the "revival of qualitative content analysis, to understand what various news media say, show, assume, and value about a range of major issues and institutions in U.S. life" (Gans 1983:181). It is in this spirit that the present study has been conducted.

The literary/linguistic analysis utilized here was intended to permit the penetration of the latent meanings of a text and "preserve something of the complexity of language and connotation which has to be sacrificed in content analysis in order to achieve high validation." Content analysis uses an initial soaking in the material to be examined "to define the categories and build a code (based on an intuitive sense of where the main clusters occur), whereas literary, stylistic and linguistic analysis uses the preliminary reading to select representative examples which can be more intensively analyzed" (Hall 1975:15).

It would be a mistake to assume that because content analysis uses precise criteria for coding evidence that it is therefore objective, while literary/linguistic analysis, which avoids such coding, is merely intuitive, invalid and/or unreliable. Literary/linguistic analyses employ evidence as

> they indicate more briefly the fuller supporting or contextual evidence which lies to hand; they take into account material which modifies or disproves the hypotheses which are emerging; and they *should* (they do not always) indicate in detail why one rather than another reading of the material seems to the analyst the most plausible way of understanding it. Content analysis assumes repetition—the pile-up of material under one of the categories—to be the most useful indicator of significance. (Hall 1975:15)

The simple count of the repetition of words, phrases, or references will not provide an understanding of the inference or meaning or vision of the world communicated by the press. Such a count, of course, should not be intended, according to its practitioners, to replace the subsequent analysis of data that is necessary, but it is the point of critics of such an approach to content analysis that the counting itself can (must) misdirect a study of the press. Literary analysis made possible the recognition and appreciation of the change of frames used by the *Times* to report Solidarity and events in Poland while the sources and references might have continued in an uninterrupted pattern. Literary/linguistic analysis permits the recognition of multiple dimensions of presentation that provides a fuller sense of the media message. Such analysis provides

> strategies for noting and taking account of emphasis. Position, placing, treatment, tone, stylistic intensification, striking imagery, etc., are all ways of registering emphasis. The really significant item may not be the one which continually recurs, but the one which stands out as the exception from the general pattern—but which is *also* given, in its exceptional context, the greatest weight. (Hall 1975:15)

An excellent example of how the exceptional is particularly telling and would be missed in a quantitative content analysis is the September 7 article in the *Globe and Mail* that reported the analysis of Ernest Volkman, the editor of *Defence Science Magazine*, suggesting that civilian air flights were frequently used by the West to gather intelligence. The article would appear as a simple hash mark on a tally sheet of content analysis, along with some other sources or articles that might indicate that the *Globe and Mail* more commonly included sources that provided information conflicting with Washington's description of events. The significance of the piece, however, is not simply that it provided a single unit of evidence about the relative balance of sources, but, instead, that an article such as that appeared at all in the Canadian newspapers while it did not, and could not, appear in the *New York Times*. There was no place for such an article in the reporting that characterized the *Times*. Editors, reporters, regular readers of the *Times*, and most Americans would have, no doubt, understood Volkman to be an irresponsible extremist to have made such unqualified assertions that conflicted with and even denied Washington's claims. The significance of the article is, again, that there was room in the Canadian political culture for it to appear in a national newspaper, but it was excluded by American political culture from finding a place in a respected American newspaper.

Similarly, literary/linguistic analysis made it possible to recognize and explain the change of frame used in the *Times* to present Solidarity during the last months of 1980. Solidarity's change from a favored, anti-communist movement to a threat to the balance of power in Europe did not require a change in news sources. A count of positive and negative adjectives might have alerted a researcher to a change that had occurred, but a reading of the sort required by literary/linguistic analysis would have been necessary to understand the change and its significance.

The choice of method of analysis was intended to permit the fullest understanding of how hegemonic ideology, or world view, influences the identification, definition and presentation of news. That presentation can, in turn, serve to either/both bolster or/and undermine the order supported by the hegemony. Literary/lingistic analysis has enabled the identification of news's hegemonic influences and the inconsistencies that can be the source of counter-hegemonies.

REFERENCES

Gans, Herbert J. (1983) "News Media, News Policy, and Democracy: Research for the Future," *Journal of Communication* 33:174–84.

Garnham, Nicholas (1983) "Toward a Theory of Cultural Materialism," *Journal of Communication* 33:314–29.

Hall, Stuart (1975) "Introduction," in *Paper Voices: The Popular Press and Social Change, 1935–1965*, A.C.H. Smith (London: Chatto and Windus), pp. 11–24.

Tuchman, Gaye (1980) "The Facts of the Moment: The Study of News," *Symbolic Interaction* 3:9–20.

SELECTED BIBLIOGRAPHY

Altheide, David L. 1984. "Media Hegemony, A Failure of a Perspective." *Public Opinion Quarterly* 48:476–90.
Anderson, Digby C., and W. W. Sharrock. 1979. "Biassing the News: Technical Issues in 'Media Studies.' " *Sociology* 30:367–85.
Bennett, Tony. 1982a. "Media, 'reality,' signification." In *Culture, Society and the Media*, edited by Michael Gurevitch, Tony Bennett, James Curran, and Janet Woollacott, 287–308. London: Methuen.
———. 1982b. "Theories of the Media, Theories of Society." In *Culture, Society and the Media*, edited by Michael Gurevitch, Tony Bennett, James Curran, and Janet Woollacott, 30–55. London: Methuen.
Blumler, Jay G. 1978. "The Social Purpose of Mass Communication Research: A Transatlantic Perspective." *Journalism Quarterly* 55:219–30.
———. 1983. "Communication and Democracy: The Crisis Beyond and the Ferment Within." *Journal of Communication* 33:166–73.
Blumler, Jay G., and Michael Gurevitch. 1982. "The Political Effects of Mass Communication." In *Culture, Society and the Media*, edited by Michael Gurevitch, Tony Bennett, James Curran, and Janet Woollacott, 236–67. London, Methuen.
Breed, Walter. 1955. "Social Control in the Newsroom." *Social Forces* 33:326–35.
Curran, James, Michael Gurevitch, and Janet Woollacott. 1982. "The Study of the Media: Theoretical Approaches." In *Culture, Society and the Media*, edited by Michael Gurevitch, Tony Bennett, James Curran, and Janet Woollacott, 11–29. London: Methuen.
Dreier, Peter. 1982. "The Position of the Press in the U.S. Power Structure." *Social Problems* 29:298–310.
Epstein, Edward Jay. 1981. "The Selection of Reality." In *What's News: The Media in*

American Society, edited by Elie Abel, 119–32. San Francisco, CA: Institute for Contemporary Studies.
Fejes, Fred. 1984. "Critical Mass Communication Research and Media Effects: The Problem of the Disappearing Audience." *Media, Culture and Society* 6:219–32.
Gans, Herbert J. 1972. "The Famine in American Mass Communication Research: Comments on Hirsch, Ischman and Gecas." *American Journal of Sociology* 77:219–32.
———. 1979. *Deciding What's News*. New York: Random House.
Gitlin, Todd. 1978. "Media Sociology: The Dominant Paradigm." *Theory and Society* 6:205–53.
———. 1980. *The Whole World Is Watching*. Berkeley, CA: University of California Press.
Glasgow Media Group. 1980. *More Bad News*. London: Routledge and Kegan Paul.
———. 1982. *Really Bad News*. London: Writers and Readers.
Gramsci, Antonio. 1971. *Selections from the Prison Notebooks*. New York: International Publications.
Hall, Stuart. 1975. "Introduction." In *Paper Voices: The Popular Press and Social Change, 1935–1965*, A.C.H. Smith, 11–24. London: Chatto and Windus.
———. 1982. "The Rediscovery of Ideology: Return of the Repressed in Media Studies." In *Culture, Society and the Media*, edited by Michael Gurevitch, Tony Bennett, James Curran, and Janet Woollacott, 56–90. London: Methuen.
Klapper, Joseph. 1960. *The Effects of Mass Communication*. Glencoe, IL: Free Press.
Knight, Graham. 1982. "News and Ideology." *Canadian Journal of Communication* 8:61–79.
Lazarsfeld, Paul F. 1941. "Remarks on Administrative and Critical Communications Research." *Studies in Philosophy and Social Science* 9:2–16.
Lukes, Steven. 1974. *Power: A Radical View*. London: Macmillan.
McQuail, Denis. 1985. "Sociology of Mass Communication." *Annual Review of Sociology* 11:93–111.
Melody, William H., and Robert E. Mansell. 1983. "The Debate Over Critical vs. Administrative Research: Circularity or Challenge." *Journal of Communication* 33:103–16.
Molotch, Harvey, and Marilyn Lester. 1974. "News as Purposeful Behavior: On the Strategic Use of Routine Events, Accidents, and Scandals." *American Sociological Review* 39:101–12.
Murdock, Graham. 1980. "Misrepresenting Media Sociology: A Reply to Anderson and Sharrock." *Sociology* 14:457–68.
Rosengren, Karl Eric. 1979. "Bias in News: Methods and Concepts." *Studies of Broadcasting* 15:31–45.
Scanlon, T. Joseph. 1972. "A New Approach to the Study of Newspaper Accuracy." *Journalism Quarterly* 49:587–90.
Schiller, Dan. 1981. *Objectivity and the News: The Public and the Rise of Commercial Journalism*. Philadelphia, PA: University of Pennsylvania Press.
Schudson, Michael. 1978. *Discovering the News: A Social History of American Newspapers*. New York: Basic Books.
Slack, Jennifer Daryl, and Martin Allar. 1983. "The Political and Epistemological Constituents of Critical Communication Research." *Journal of Communication* 33:208–18.

Stevenson, Robert L. 1983. "A Critical Look at Critical Analysis."*Journal of Communication* 33:262–69.
Stevenson, Robert L., and Mark T. Greene. 1980. "A Reconstruction of Bias in the News." *Journalism Quarterly* 57:115–21.
Tuchman, Gaye. 1972. "Objectivity as Strategic Ritual: An Examination of Newsmen's Notions of Objectivity." *American Journal of Sociology* 77:660–79.
White, David M. 1950. "The Gatekeeper: A Case Study in the Selection of News." *Journalism Quarterly* 27:383–90.

INDEX

administrative studies/research, 14
Aeroflot, 42
agenda setting, 20
Apple, R. W., Jr., 108, 110, 111
Associated Press, 52, 57, 89, 118
Austin, Anthony, 106

behaviorism/behavioral, 9, 18, 19, 22, 23, 26, 27, 28, 30
Brzezinski, Zbigniew, 113
Bulletin of Concerned Asian Scientists, 75
Burt, Richard, 65, 72

capitalism/capitalist, 2, 25, 140, 141
Carter, Jimmy (President), 111, 112, 113, 116
Catto, Henry, E., 71, 72, 75
Central Intelligence Agency (CIA), 59
coercion, 25
consensus, 2, 17, 18, 20, 22, 24, 25, 63, 128
counter hegemonic, 37, 43, 92, 114, 132, 142
critical studies/paradigm, 15, 16, 17, 26, 127

cultural studies, 15, 16, 17
culture, political, 3, 4, 36, 37, 49, 85, 86, 92, 93, 106, 126, 129, 132, 134, 139, 142

Darnton, John, 1, 106, 107, 114, 115, 116, 118, 129
Defence Science Magazine, 84, 86, 142
Defence Weekly, 80
democracy, 1, 2, 4, 5, 6, 25, 34, 36, 37, 133, 134
Department of Defense, 78
dependency model, 20
Downie, Leonard Jr., 73, 78

empirical/empiricism, 15, 16, 17, 18, 19, 141

fact/facts, 5, 7, 12, 40, 59, 73, 80, 97, 114, 124, 125, 126
fair/fairness, 10, 13, 14, 126
frame(s), 3, 13, 29, 51, 56, 58, 67, 69, 70, 86, 93, 94, 97, 103, 104, 108, 119, 124, 128, 129, 130, 132, 140, 142

gatekeeper/gatekeeper studies, 27, 30
Gdansk/Gdansk shipyard, 99, 102, 115
Gelb, Leslie H., 53, 63, 64
Gierek, Wladyslaw, 102, 103
Globe and Mail, 78, 82, 83, 84, 85, 86, 140, 141, 142
Gomulka, Wladyslaw, 102
Gromyko, Andrei, 105
Gwertman, Bernard, 112, 113, 114, 115, 116

hegemony/hegemonic, 3, 4, 24, 25, 26, 29, 36, 37, 43, 76, 85, 94, 106, 112, 113, 114, 119, 126, 127, 128, 130, 131, 132, 134, 140, 142

ideology/ideological, 3, 13, 14, 15, 16, 17, 18, 24, 25, 26, 27, 28, 37, 76, 85, 94, 113, 128, 130, 131, 132, 134, 142
Immen, Wallace, 85, 86
Inman, Bobby R. (Admiral), 72
Interfactory Strike Committee, 99
Internat'l Civic Aviation Org. (ICAO), 55, 70, 71, 72, 74, 75

Japanese Air Force, 52, 57, 59, 60
Japanese radar, 39, 63
journalism, 3, 5, 6, 7, 8, 11, 12, 14, 29, 71, 86, 88, 92, 109, 125, 127, 133, 139, 140; advocacy, 35
journalists, 1, 3, 5, 6, 7, 8, 9, 10, 11, 12, 13, 23, 26, 27, 28, 29, 30, 43, 46, 47, 52, 55, 56, 60, 61, 65, 75, 76, 77, 78, 80, 84, 86, 88, 91, 92, 93, 99, 101, 102, 107, 108, 110, 111, 112, 120, 125, 126, 127, 130, 134

Kania, Stanislaw, 103, 106, 107, 109, 110, 114
knowledge gap, 21, 23
Kuron, Jacek, 102, 118, 131

legitimacy, 10, 13, 14, 20, 24, 25, 70, 81, 86, 129, 133
Lenin Shipyard, 99

Maclean's, 78, 79, 80, 81, 82, 86, 140, 141

mass society, 15, 19
McDonald, Lawrence P., 38, 82
media organizations, 27, 30
methodology/methodological, 15, 18, 23, 28, 141
Middleton, Drew, 85, 86, 116
mirror theory, 12
Muskie, Edmund, 111, 113, 116

The Nation, 70, 71, 72, 73, 74, 76, 77, 90, 92
nationalism/nationalist, 130, 140
National Security Agency (NSA), 41, 57, 59, 70, 72, 113
National Transportation Safety Board, 75
navigational equipment/systems, 39, 53, 54, 55, 79
Nixon, Richard, 98, 119, 120

Ogarkov, Nikolai, 45, 89
ontology/ontological, 21, 22, 23, 26
operationalize/operationalization, 10, 11, 18, 26

patriotism, 5, 139
Pearson, David, 71, 77, 78, 90
pluralism/pluralist, 4, 14, 15, 17, 18, 19, 21, 22, 23, 26, 35, 40
positivism, 18, 141
power elite, 21, 23, 26
press: commercial, 35; free, 3, 4, 5, 6, 35, 36, 37, 71, 78, 85, 92, 139, 140; state-controlled, 35, 36, 92, 139, 140
propaganda, 15, 129
public opinion, 19, 20, 89

Reagan, Ronald, 38, 40, 44, 45, 53, 62, 64, 68, 69, 71, 74, 75, 81, 83, 87, 89
reality, 8, 9, 11, 12, 13, 14, 22, 24, 25, 27, 28, 37, 44, 61, 76, 92, 94, 120, 125, 127, 128, 130
reconnaissance plane (RC–135), 42, 45, 48, 49, 51, 57, 58, 60, 69, 72, 75, 85, 90

Sakhalin/Sakhalin Island, 46, 52, 62, 78, 82, 89, 90
Shultz, George, 64, 65, 79, 83

socialization, 1
Soviet Foreign Ministry, 111
spiral of silence, 20
State Department, 50, 61, 65, 67, 69, 82, 83, 87, 108, 109, 115, 116
Sudan, 124
Sudan Airways, 19
Sudanese People's Liberation Army, 19

Tass, 45, 83, 87, 88, 89, 90, 92, 114, 115

Taubman, Phillip, 72, 73
totality, 3, 27, 28, 134

Volkman, Ernest, 84, 85, 86, 142

Walesa, Lech, 100, 101, 115, 131
Washington Journalism Review, 71
Washington Post, 73, 74, 78
Witkin, Richard, 55

About the Author

ALLAN RACHLIN is an Assistant Professor of sociology at Bradford College, Massachusetts. He earned his Ph.D. at the State University of New York at Buffalo, where he has also held a Visiting Faculty position. One of his primary research interests is the mutually formative relationship or interpenetration of political culture, in its variety of expressions, and societal order.

E 389.5 .R34 1988

	DATE DUE		
OCT 04 1991			
SEP 22 1992			